"*Surviving Production is an invaluable and comprehensive guide for production coordinators. Deborah Patz has drawn on her own experience and has written a thoroughly researched and helpful book.*"

Norman Jewison,
Film producer and director

"*This book is the Swiss Army knife of production management!*"

Rob Mills

President, Radical Sheep Productions

"*This book should be mandatory reading in our industry. Patz has covered every aspect of filmmaking from a coordinator's point of view. This book should be the bible for all beginners and all those who aren't quite sure how things work. Well done!*"

Alex Beaton,
MCA, Executive in Charge of Production, Action Network

"*Incredibly detailed and thorough . . .*"

Mark Shivas, Head of Films, BBC

"*This generous book leaves no stone unturned as Patz takes the reader on a comprehensive journey from prep to post.*"

Ann Marie Fleming
Independent Filmmaker

"*An extremely comprehensive practical guide, written with insight and humor.*"

Alexandra Raffé
Producer, *I've Heard the Mermaids Singing*

D0187840

SURVIVING
PRODUCTION

THE ART OF PRODUCTION MANAGEMENT
FOR FILM AND TELEVISION

DEBORAH S. PATZ

For Laura

who was there at the beginning

Published by Michael Wiese Productions, 11288 Ventura Blvd., Suite 821, Studio City, CA 91604 (818) 379-8799 Fax (818) 986-3408.
E-mail: wiese@earthlink.net
http://websites.earthlink.net/~mwp

Cover design by Wade Lageose, Art Hotel, Los Angeles
Copy Editing by Bernice Balfour
Page Layout by Kathleen Crislip and Patti Rawlins

Printed by Braun-Brumfield, Inc., Ann Arbor, Michigan
Manufactured in the United States of America

Copyright 1997 by Deborah S. Patz

All rights reserved. No part of this book may be reproduced in any form or by any means without permission in writing from the author, except for the inclusion of brief quotations in a review.

Note: The information presented in this book is for education purposes only. The authors are not giving business or financial advice. Readers should consult their lawyers, accountants and financial advisors on their budgets. The publisher is not liable for how readers may choose to use this information.

Library of Congress Cataloging in Publication Data

Patz, Deborah S.

Surviving Production: the art of production management for film and television / Deborah S. Patz.
    p.   cm.
    ISBN 0-941188-60-4
    1. Motion pictures--Production and direction. 2. Television--Production and direction. I. Title
PN1995.9.P7W45   1996
791.43'0233--dc20   96-25539
                                                                          CIP

Books from
MICHAEL WIESE PRODUCTIONS

Surviving Production
Persistence of Vision
Directing Actors
Film & Video on the Internet
The Digital Videomaker's Guide
Shaking the Money Tree
The Writer's Journey
Film Directing: Shot by Shot
Film Directing: Cinematic Motion
Fade In: The Screenwriting Process
The Writer's Journey
Producer to Producer
Film & Video Financing
Film & Video Marketing
Film & Video Budgets
The Independent Film & Videomaker's Guide

TABLE OF CONTENTS

ACKNOWLEDGMENTS

There are so many wonderful people and companies to thank, since this industry is very much a team sport. Beyond all the crews I have worked with over the years that have given me, and continue to give me, the forum to learn so much about filmmaking, I must acknowledge with great thanks:

Michael Wiese and Ken Lee for making this project come to life, and especially Michael for reading his e–mail. Victoria Ridout at the Writer's Union of Canada for her work beyond the call of duty.

Cheryl Wagner, Rob Mills, and Nadine Henry of Radical Sheep Productions for their support when it really counted. Seaton McLean, Jamie Paul Rock, and John Calvert for my many precious years at Atlantis. The Canadian Film Centre for creating a terrific testing ground for the book. My many wonderful assistants over the years without whose dedication, survival would have been impossible.

Sue Phillips for seeing my abilities before I did. Ann Marie Fleming for never letting me forget them.

Scott Baker for buying me the book that got the ball rolling. Francis Fougere and his flying f-stops for the lovely photograph. And Nick DeMunnik for security of "plan B."

My team of readers and critics for their invaluable input: Paul Bernard, Trish Brown, Laura Fisher, Lon Hall, Danny McCoy, Richard Patz, Joan Pearce, Melissa from O'Reilly, Dean & Power, Cesar from Packair, and Clive from Renown Freight Limited.

My mother and father for the inspiration to succeed at whatever my heart desires and for their unending love and support.

And finally, my deepest thanks go to Mo Patz and Kathryn Emslie without whose help this book could never have been completed.

INTRODUCTION

A film production explodes from paper agreement into life as a thriving expanse of business. Propelling itself forward in a frantic race against time, it captures on tape or celluloid a collaboration of ideas — entertaining, thrilling, and educating. But before audiences see the final product, production has long since vanished. Crews are working with different people on other projects. The production office now houses another business or lies empty. There is no trace left of the company that made it all happen, save the telephone message that says the number has changed to head office.

In that brief existence of time, and under such frenetic circumstances, a film is made. This book is a survival guide for the hands–on management of a film shoot for the production office. It is told through the eyes of the person in the office who arranges it all, does it all, double–checks it all: the Production Coordinator.

The Production Coordinator deals with everyone and everything during the course of making a film, from pre-production to post-production, at head office and on set. If you think it sounds like an enormous job, it is. Filled with the excitement of being in the center of everything, the job is also weighted with responsibilities. Good Production Coordinators are hailed as people who "keep the show running." They have secrets on how to do the job effectively that tend to remain just that — secrets. This book is written to share those secrets.

True production stories are interspersed with straightforward "how-to" directions. Beyond entertaining, the stories are intended to balance out the simplicity of organizing in the void of the pages of a book. See how real life situations happen. Production Coordinators are not perfect. Their daily accomplishments may make them appear superhuman, but Coordinators are just like you and me.

Knowledge and understanding of the office's expanse of responsibilities can only help production to proceed with trust, good humor, and a sense of teamwork. Together you are responsible for everything in this book.

Production Secretaries, Production Assistants, and Receptionists will also deem this book invaluable. Be familiar with the scope of duties that you accomplish together in the production office. Bring meaning to and put into perspective the work that you do.

As well, those entering the film industry will learn about the business side of filmmaking from this book. Since the Coordinator deals with everyone from prep to post, you can acquaint yourself with an overview of the entire film production process.

Finally, this book is for those in, and interested in, the film industry who are baffled by what the Production Coordinator actually does. They are the ones who ask, "How can a person be that busy?"

So, grab your life jacket and enter the world of filmmaking. Survive a film production in the shoes of the busiest person on the crew: the Production Coordinator. It is a full production experience, and no other job can compare to it.

PRE-PRODUCTION

Interview Novices

Going for my first interview as a Production Coordinator, I was very nervous. I had noted down on a cue card in tiny writing all the questions I could muster about the show and my prospective role in production. What I didn't know at the time was that I was being interviewed by a relatively new Production Manager.

He asked me a few general questions. I stumbled out a few answers. Silences and uncomfortable moments crept into the interview. Now and then, I referred to my cue card and asked a question myself. The Production Manager was intrigued by the card in my hand. He leaned forward to get a glimpse of its contents, and then said, "You seem more prepared for this than I. Why don't you take over the interview?" I realized now that he was as nervous as I about this whole matter. So I blatantly referred to my cue card and continued with my questions, jotting down answers as we discussed the different topics. Soon conversation was lively, direct, and informative. He leaned back in comfort and we lost track of time chatting about film, the project, and the workings of a production office.

By the next day I was working in that office. Interestingly, it occurred to me that the only question I didn't ask him at the time was "Did I get the job?"

FIRST QUESTIONS FIRST

At the Interview or on the First Day

Congratulations! You made it to the job interview. The conversation and chitchat are going well. You are beginning to relax as you do your best to show that you are amply experienced and professional for the job, while still trying to demonstrate that you are a fun co-worker. Then the Production Manager asks if you have any questions. Immediately every thought that was beginning to settle in your mind disappears in a puff of smoke, and you sit there totally blank. No amount of trying will bring back those questions you know you had. You cannot remember a single one. You begin to sweat.

A. INTERVIEW QUESTIONS

Bring a pen, paper, and cue cards into the interview. As a Production Coordinator, you are being hired to organize not to memorize. This is your opportunity to be organized in the interview. On the job you will be walking around with pen and paper anyway, so get into the habit now. Here are eighteen questions you will want written on the cue cards for during the interview:

1. What Are The Shooting Start And End Dates?
This will be the first question the crew will ask of you.

2. Do You Expect To Have Weekend Shoots Or 6-Day Workweeks?
Some films schedule their workweek to include shooting on Saturdays, Sundays, and holidays to take advantage of reduced traffic or greater location availability. If it will be a 6-day workweek, consider and adjust your fee accordingly.

3. Do You Expect To Have Long Shooting Days?

Is it planned to be a 9-hour day or 12-hour day? The film will be budgeted to shoot a certain minimum number of hours per day. Note that lunch hour is not included in describing the day's length, so a 9-hour day plus lunch is actually 10 hours long.

4. What Hours Do You Like The Office Open?

Some Production Managers insist that the office be open at least 30 minutes prior to call time until 30 minutes after wrap with prep and wrap days being a minimum of 9:00 a.m. to 6:00 p.m. Some Production Managers will leave the office opening schedule up to you.

5. Will The Film Have "Day Shoots" And/Or "Night Shoots"?

On night shoots, some Production Managers prefer to have the office open both business hours (9:00 a.m. to 6:00 p.m.) and set hours (all night long). If this is the case, you will need extra office crew to make it happen. Discuss this now.

6. How Elaborate Is The Shoot?

The Production Manager may ask what you mean by this. Will there be a lot of extras, locations, special effects, music clearances? This question is designed to help you determine how complex your job is going to be.

7. Will There Be Any Actors Or Crew From Out Of Town?

This question will determine how much you will need to deal with travel agents and immigration.

8. Who Is The Film For?

Another question the crew will have for you right away, is for you to find out who is broadcasting the show, or which distributor is handling the feature.

9. Who Are The Producers? How Many Are There? How Involved Are They?

Executives can come from many different companies and countries to make up the list of producers for a film. There can be Executive Producers, Supervising Producers, Associate Producers, Creative Producers, Producers, Co-Producers, Line Producers, or any other "Producer" title newly invented. Since the titles are not standard for describing the duties of each position, here you can find out how each producer is involved and in what political order to list them on the crew list. As subtext, you will also learn how big a job your paperwork distribution to the various companies will be, and may get an idea of how long head office decisions will take by determining how active each of the various producers intends to be.

10. What Is The Company Name For This Film Production?

Film companies set up separate incorporated companies for each film production for legal and accounting purposes. You need to know this name to conduct any business, from making letterheads to setting up accounts and contracts.

11. Where Are The Production Offices? How Set Up Are They?

Some offices are simply empty rooms that you have to furnish from scratch. Others are fully furnished right down to telephone systems and photocopiers. This question will determine how busy you will be in your first few days.

12. Do You Have A Computer System Already? What Kind Is It?

Often the Production Coordinator comes to a production with a computer. If you do, negotiate a kit rental fee and find out if your system or training is compatible with the company's.

13. Do You Have Corporate Accounts Already Established?

Some companies prefer you to use their head office courier, photocopier, office stationery accounts, etc., whereas others encourage you to bring in your own contacts.

14. What Production Paper Work Do You Require? Any Preferred Forms?

These questions are merely confirmation that the Production Manager wants completed production reports, call sheets, production schedules, and so on. Though redundant, they should spark further discussion about any existing forms the company prefers to use, and who, between the Assistant Directors and you, will be responsible for certain paperwork. You will also learn how easy it is to talk to the Production Manager and how much the P.M. will rely on you for the correct paperwork on the show.

15. How Much Of The Crew Has Been Hired?

Here is where your pen and paper prove useful. Write down all names and positions the Production Manager mentions. Also note the status of each person. Often names will be chosen for the various positions, but not confirmed yet. Be aware of who may come on board, but never publish any unconfirmed information on a crew list. This is your opportunity to show how you deal with confidential information.

16. How Many Staff Will Be In The Office?

Find out how much the budget allows for a Production Secretary and assistants. Also find out if you will be hiring the assistants, or you will have assistants appointed to you. Some assistant roles may be already hired or promised by producers, managers, or executives prior to your arrival.

17. How Soon Do You Want The Production Coordinator To Start?

This will be a budgetary concern for the Production Manager. Be prepared if the date is tomorrow.

18. What Is In The Budget For The Production Coordinator?

This is the dance of the numbers. You ask the Production Manager how much is in the budget, the Production Manager asks you how much you expect to make. If the Coordinator job is union, the dance can be short as you can look up the scale rate to start, but if the job is nonunion, the price range is enormous. Consider the scale and budget of the film together with your research from other Coordinators to determine a starting price, if you intend to jump in with the first number. Remember to negotiate your computer and equipment kit rental separately.

B. INTERVIEW TANGENTS

Do not be afraid of tangents. These questions are intended to spark plenty of conversation and further questions between you and the Production Manager. Go ahead and discuss the film in more detail. You two will be spending a lot of time together, so get to know each other. Keep in mind how much time you have for this meeting to determine when to bring the conversation back on track. You may not be able to get all the answers right away. That is okay. You can leave some of the questions for the first day of the job.

C. AFTER THE INTERVIEW

You do not have to decide to take the job at the interview. The Production Manager may be interviewing other candidates and will want to make a decision later. You are welcome to think about the possible job overnight, too. Later, review your cue cards and notes. Do you want to get involved with this job? It will be a huge commitment. Seriously think about it. Sleep on it. Follow up with the Production Manager the next day.

D. ABOUT THE PRODUCTION COORDINATOR AND THE PRODUCTION MANAGER

Have everything you do overseen by the Production Manager. This may seem a slow process at first, but as you develop a relationship of trust with that Production Manager, you will be given a greater forum to initiate and act, unsupervised. Never forget to inform the Production Manager of what is happening. The P.M. needs to know as much as you about what is happening in the making of the film. At its best, you and the P.M. will become friends and trust each other with secrets that will help both of you in excelling at your respective jobs. At its worst, you and the P.M. will not inform nor help each other, and the production will stumble along with great problems as everyone finds out crucial information after the fact. Communication is a two-way street, so start off your side as best as you can.

* * *

Congratulations! You made it to the end of the interview! You have been hired to coordinate a film! Celebrate. Take yourself out for dinner and a movie. After today, you are going to spend an awful lot of your time and effort on the production. The real adventure is about to begin. You are about to walk into an empty set of rooms and turn them into a running film production office. Armed with all the answers you acquired during the interview, you are ready.

SWEATY THE BURGLAR

Most break-ins are memorable for the grief they cause. Critical office equipment is stolen, yet you must continue with production at the same frantic pace. You feel an invasion of privacy knowing that someone was in the office routing through your things in your absence. You are not alone.

Well, my most memorable break-in was by a fellow we never caught. This was a fellow that we didn't even know broke into and out of the office four times, until a month after he'd done so. He left no trace of his presence and took no office equipment of any kind. Yet a month after his first deed we had an exact record of his movements and written proof. At this point, I dubbed him "Sweaty" because this is what he was up to: Sweaty broke into the production office every Thursday morning precisely at 2:00 a.m. Each time he came in, he used our office for a solid three hours. He spent his time dialing and redialing "1-900" phone-sex numbers.

We never discovered the way Sweaty got into the office, and by the second month, he was gone and never returned. His signature? He left us his $750 telephone bill!

THE BIG SETUP

Setting Up The Production Office

You wake up at home. You think about the responsibility that is about to start today when you go to work to turn an empty office into a production office and once the film is done, make the office empty again. Turn to your bedside table. This is where you start. Put a pen and paper beside the bed. This is for when you wake up in the middle of the night panicked that you have to remember to do something in the office the next day. Next set up two alarm clocks (one battery operated) so that no matter how tired you are, and no matter what power outage happens, you can wake up on time. Finally, go into the office, open the book to this chapter, and begin.

A. MAPPING OUT THE OFFICE

You have an empty office and a group of people that will be using it. Your first order of business is to place everyone logically in that office. Draw out a rough sketch of the office floor plan. Your artistic skills are not at test here, so have fun with it.

1. Draw The Office Floor Plan

The office likely will have a large open area and several smaller offices with doors and locks. Do not worry about creating an exceptional quality drawing or even a floor plan to scale, but do note which offices are larger than others and which ones have windows. You will use this map extensively in this chapter, and again for marking the placement of telephone extensions, so "legible" is the only keyword.

2. List Crew Who Will Need Offices And/Or Desks

Make a list of who will be using the office, who needs a desk, who needs a lockable room, and who has already been assigned a desk or room. Get input from the Production Manager for accuracy.

3. Place Names On The Floor Plan

With pencil and eraser, or with names marked on Post-it notes, place the crew on the floor plan. Talk to each department for their wish list regarding office placement. Move the names around and around until you achieve an appropriate compromise for all wishes. Using a modest film as an example, here are some likely initial minimum concerns about crew placement:

- Producer — private office

- Director — private office

- Production Manager — private office; near Production Coordinator — for frequent access

- Production Accountant — private office that locks

- Production Secretary — near entrance door to act as reception

- Production Coordinator — near the entrance if there is no Secretary; in a place of high traffic, so that crew and Coordinator have frequent access to each other

- Office Production Assistant — desk

- Assistant Director Department — desk and telephone; near Director

- Locations Department — room for maps on walls; room for storage   of tables, chairs, and other locations purchases

- Art Department — room for drafting tables and large filing cabinets

- Set Dressing Department — room for storage of purchases

- Wardrobe Department — room for wardrobe racks and wardrobe purchases; dressing rooms and fitting room for studio shoot; laundry   room

- Hair/Makeup Department — room with makeup mirror for studio shoot

- Transportation Department — desk and telephone

4. Place Large Furniture And Equipment On Floor Plan

Once the crew is placed, make a list of required furniture to be rented or purchased. Approve the list by the Production Manager, then order the furniture immediately. While you wait for the furniture to arrive, use pencil and eraser or more Post-it notes to add further decorating concerns to your office map.

THE LARGE FURNITURE AND EQUIPMENT CHECKLIST

- ☐ Photocopier
- ☐ Fax Machine
- ☐ Photocopier and Fax Machine Supplies
- ☐ Office Supplies — Photocopier Paper Storage Shelf
- ☐ Office Supplies — Stationery Shelf/Cabinet
- ☐ Filing Cabinets
- ☐ Television and VCR (Office)
- ☐ VCR (Producer or Director)
- ☐ Office Craft Service Area
- ☐ Water Cooler
- ☐ Washer/Dryer
- ☐ Distribution Table
- ☐ Wall Envelopes (Crew)
- ☐ Wall Envelopes (Companies)
- ☐ Wall Envelopes (Forms)
- ☐ "To Set" Box
- ☐ "To Head Office" Box
- ☐ "P.A." Box
- ☐ "Mail" Box
- ☐ Rushes/Dailies Sign

PHOTOCOPIER

You will be making up to about 10,000 copies per week. Honestly. Rent the best high volume and fastest machine you can. This means you will be getting a loud machine, so do not place the photocopier next to the reception telephone. Put it in its own room, or at least in the most remote place in the office with dividers around it for sound containment. You will be double-sided copying the call sheet, collating masses of scripts, copying on letter-size, legal-size, 11x17 size (for the art department), enlarging and shrinking, and clearing out paper jams with great frequency. Some companies will loan you a second machine at no charge to have on hand in case the main photocopier breaks down (which it usually does on Fridays after 5:00 p.m.). Get a service contract.

FAX MACHINE

This is the second most popular machine in the office. If you can afford a plain paper fax, it is worth the money — imagine getting a 120-page script by fax minutes before shooting, and having to photocopy every curly page for the 75 crew and cast. This machine is not loud. Keep it accessible so that you and/or the Secretary can monitor it from your desks.

PHOTOCOPIER AND FAX MACHINE SUPPLIES

Both machines need toner and paper. Store these supplies near each machine for efficiency of replacement and for frequency of monitoring them. Supplies can come from your office supplies source, from an independent source, or be included in your service contract. Check around for best rates and accessibility.

OFFICE SUPPLIES — PHOTOCOPIER PAPER STORAGE SHELVES

Have plenty of shelving available for the various colors of paper you will need for script revisions. Store them near the photocopier for ease of access. Label each shelf for each color and stack the reams of paper so that at a glance you can see which colored paper is running low.

OFFICE SUPPLIES — STATIONERY SHELF/CABINET

Place a cabinet or shelf in a visible area of the office for storage of all the supplies. Have a pen and paper (preferably attached to each other) on hand for crew requests. Make sure there is a space on that paper for crew to note their request and their name so that the right supplies get to the right people. The Production Manager will approve the requests before ordering to prevent crew overindulgence. Many companies deliver office supplies. It is a great way to cut down on the Office Production Assistant's runs. Check how long the turnaround for an order is, what conditions are inflicted on the order, and if the price makes it worthwhile.

FILING CABINETS

Note who will require them, from the Producer to the Production Manager to the Production Accountant to yourself. The top of a two-drawer lateral filing cabinet can serve a great second purpose as a shelf for the facsimile machine or a set of binders. An empty filing cabinet drawer can serve as a locking drawer for supplies you or the Accountant will need hidden and secure.

TELEVISION AND VCR (OFFICE)

If production is going to have video rushes, a VCR and television for the office are essential. Discuss with the Production Manager which features you will need and how long you will need the equipment. Shop around, because depending on the term of use, renting or buying will be the better option. Remember to get a stand with or without wheels for the equipment, and decide if it is going to be kept in the Producer's or Director's office, or in the main office (for everyone's access). Remember to get plenty of extension cords and patch cords.

VCR (PRODUCER OR DIRECTOR)

Visiting Producers or Directors may need a VCR in their hotel rooms. Check with the Production Manager. A second VCR in the office (when not at the hotel) can be used to dub rushes and final shows.

OFFICE CRAFT SERVICE AREA

Often this area is where the office television and VCR are kept. Impromptu meetings happen here as people meet each other over a cup of coffee. Place a couch or a few chairs in this spot to make the area more like a lounge or waiting area. Use a coffee table, end tables, lamps, and posters as other decorating ideas. Be creative. Set up the food and drink section with some or all of the following:

> • Coffee Machine — so mandatory, the coffee machine could be a union requirement; keep in mind you will be ordering a second one for use on set.

> • Tea Kettle — good for instant soup, hot chocolate, and, of course, tea.

> • Refrigerator — to store milk, cream, brown bag lunches, and, of course, after-work beer.

> • Other Equipment — cappuccino maker, toaster, toaster oven, microwave oven, hot plate, and any other equipment your heart desires and the budget allows.

> • First Aid Kit — when shooting, the set will need one, so buy a first aid kit early for use around the office; when shooting begins, you can scale down the size of the office kit and give the big one to set.

WATER COOLER

The water cooler is just about as necessary as the coffee machine. You can choose from cold water only to hot and cold water machines. Either way, water and coffee machines have a love-hate relationship. It is not a good idea to have them next to each other. The high mineral content of bottled water creates a buildup and plugs the coffee machine in such a way that water will pour out any side crack in the coffee machine. You can check with your coffee company and find out if your machine is designed, like most, for tap water. If the crew does not like the taste of the coffee, try a new coffee bean. Also note that you will likely be ordering a second water machine for use on set.

WASHER/DRYER

The Wardrobe Department will need these. Louder and hotter than the photocopier, this duo need their own room. Check whether renting or buying makes more sense. You will need a plumber for installation.

DISTRIBUTION TABLE

Place a folding table in the highest traffic area of the office. Position it so that everyone will trip over it. You want them to do just that, because on the distribution table you will be putting all the latest paperwork that the crew wants and needs (copies of scripts, crew lists, call sheets, and so on). Make sure that you, the Secretary and/or the Office Production Assistant can see the distribution table so that you can keep the paper topped up as the hoards of crew descend on this table daily.

WALL ENVELOPES (CREW)

Assign wall space near the Secretary's or your desk for the wall envelopes. Use heavy duty envelopes, mark them for each department, and use them to gather paperwork for those departments currently not in the office. A paper-clip on front can also serve to gather their respective telephone messages. (A list of possible departments is in Chapter 18: "The Joy of Distribution.")

WALL ENVELOPES (COMPANIES)

Assign wall space for these too. Similar to the crew wall envelopes, these are used to gather paperwork for the various producing and outside companies involved. Collect paperwork over the course of the week, and send these packages at week's end. (A list of possible companies is in Chapter 18: "The Joy of Distribution.")

WALL ENVELOPES (FORMS)

Assign more wall space for these envelopes. These are blank forms that crew will ask you for constantly, from letterhead to time sheets. (A list of envelopes is in Chapter 8: "A Form for All.")

"TO SET" BOX

This box can be made out of a paper box top and placed on the distribution table, or near the entrance door. Use it to collect paper, notes, and all those various items that must go to set on the next run. Everyone (such as the Drivers and the Office Production Assistant) en route to set should check this box before leaving the office. Make it convenient for them to check.

"TO HEAD OFFICE" BOX

Like the "To Set" box, place this so that it becomes the last place to check before going to the head office. This box can be made redundant if all items to go to head office are put into the "P.A." box.

"P.A." BOX

This is the in-tray for the Office Production Assistant. Place it on the Office P.A.'s desk, and make sure it is big enough to hold parcels as well as paperwork.

"MAIL" BOX

Place this in the office to gather mail to be posted (near the "P.A." box or the "To Set" box). Ensure that each night someone takes the contents to a real mail box. Set a policy about buying stamps so that crew do not get in the habit of leaving you their unstamped mail for production to mail.

RUSHES/DAILIES SIGN

Some call them "rushes," some call them "dailies." Since "dailies" can sometimes take several days to ship and process, and "dailies" is also a term for crew members that are only working today, "rushes" is the better term. So, whatever you call the film that has just been processed and is ready for first viewing, be familiar with both terms. Make and place a sign by your desk that reads: "Rushes Tonight Will Be At" — and leave a space for the time and location. The time will change daily, and even hourly. Having it posted saves you from remembering the latest change and informs people around you without their having to interrupt and ask you.

5. List Small Equipment For Rental/Purchase

Along with all the large office furniture and equipment, there will be equipment too small to be shown on your handy office map, but can hardly be called insignificant. Before arranging for the following, address these concerns:

THE SMALL EQUIPMENT CHECKLIST

☐ Telephones

☐ Typing Equipment (Computers and Printers)

☐ Typing Equipment (Typewriters)

TELEPHONES

Make a list of who needs a telephone before you approach the telephone company. Note who really needs to have access to long distance on their set and who would just like to have it. You can restrict long distance and directory assistance on individual sets. It is amazing how many long distance calls happen on a telephone that is on an unmanned desk in an open concept office. It is also amazing how many times you will pay for directory assistance no matter how many telephone books are stacked by each telephone set. (More on choosing a telephone system is in Chapter 5: "Ring, Ring, Ring.")

TYPING EQUIPMENT — COMPUTERS and PRINTERS

Are you using Apple or IBM? Laser or bubble jet? Are you bringing in your own equipment or renting? How many people need one? Keep the name of a repair company handy.

TYPING EQUIPMENT — TYPEWRITERS

The old-fashioned typewriter is still handy for typing envelopes and checks. It is also great when you cannot afford a computer. And it is especially useful when you have a repair company name nearby.

6. Invisible Office Requirements

Your handy office map can take a break. "Invisible" office requirements are services that you must have on hand to complete the office setup. Over time you will have a contact list of these companies that you use from show to show. On your first show, take the time to start this list early — before something happens and you need a plumber at midnight!

THE INVISIBLE OFFICE REQUIREMENTS CHECKLIST

- ☐ Security (Office Alarm System)
- ☐ Security (Locations and Studio)
- ☐ Cleaners
- ☐ Plumber
- ☐ Production Assistant Car
- ☐ Keys
- ☐ Circuits and Electrician

SECURITY (OFFICE ALARM SYSTEM)

The Production Manager will likely want you to arrange for an alarm system in the office. Though film shoots are transient, unprotected computer equipment is asking for trouble for any length of time. The cost of an alarm system makes sense. You may think that replacement through insurance is adequate, but imagine working for weeks without any computer equipment until the insurance company completes the claim.

SECURITY (LOCATIONS and STUDIO)

If there is no Locations Department, you will be arranging for a security company to watch the set after hours. You can find names and references in your film reference books or from your Location Manager friend.

CLEANERS

It is usually best to arrange for them to clean the office at least twice a week.

PLUMBER

Have a plumber's name on hand. It could be the same plumber you use to install the washer/dryer. Know what hours he is accessible, especially for those after-hours bathroom jobs in old buildings.

PRODUCTION ASSISTANT CAR

The sooner you get this, the sooner the Office Production Assistant can run wildly around the city taking care of business. Well, not too wildly, you hope. Check if the Production Manager already has an account with a car rental company for the production vehicles, so that you can get the office car from the same agency. Know that you may arrange for the office car to be yours, the Secretary's, or the Office Production Assistant's car after hours.

KEYS

The Production Manager may want to change the locks when you first move in. Arrange this as soon as possible. As for how many copies you will need, start a list for one key per department head as a rough estimate. Keep a log of who gets which keys. Keys will get lost, so keep a master set for yourself.

CIRCUITS and ELECTRICIAN

Pull out the office map again. Mark on it where each wall plug is in the office. Take the time to do a circuit check and label each wall plug, the breaker panel, and the map. This is a great job to delegate to the Office Production Assistant when few people are using the office (and therefore few using the electricity). Have an electrician's name on hand for after hours. Heavy drains on a circuit are:

Photocopier. Most high volume, fast photocopiers require a dedicated circuit. That is a single wall plug that is connected to a single breaker. Have an electrician install one.

Craft Service. Any electric appliance which prepares food is a big drain on the circuit (this includes coffee machines, tea kettles, microwave ovens, refrigerators, toasters, etc.). Have an electrician install a few dedicated plugs in the craft service area.

Though this project sounds like a lot of work, this is time well spent. You do not want to find out when you turn on the coffee machine and blow a circuit someday that the Accountant's computer is sharing that same circuit.

B. SETTING UP SUPPLIER ACCOUNTS AND CONTACTS

The office map aside now, it is time to set up supplier accounts. Armed with the name of the film company and help from the Production Accountant in filling out account applications, you are ready. However, before committing to a new company right away, do a price check on three competing companies. From this process you will be able to judge how suppliers are to deal with, and how affordable they are.

THE SUPPLIER ACCOUNTS and CONTACTS CHECKLIST

- ☐ Courier Account
- ☐ Stationery Account
- ☐ Taxi Account
- ☐ Walkie-talkie Account
- ☐ Pager Account
- ☐ Cellular Phone Account
- ☐ Travel Agent
- ☐ Limousine Account
- ☐ Hotel Account
- ☐ Research Company
- ☐ Customs Broker
- ☐ Credit Card Number

COURIER ACCOUNT

You will need three couriers: a local courier, a national courier, and an international one. Some couriers can cover more than one of these needs, but beware that the price differences can be excessive in the overlapping territories.

STATIONERY ACCOUNT

Set up an account with an office supplies company that delivers, or a discount store of your choice. This will save the Office Production Assistant from keeping copious amounts of cash on hand.

TAXI ACCOUNT

Taxi account chits are simple, convenient, and often times misused. There is also an administrative cost involved in using an account; therefore the taxi charges are usually higher than if you had paid cash. Decide with the Production Manager whether or not to go with a taxi account.

WALKIE-TALKIE ACCOUNT

The Assistant Directors will have their preference about who should have walkies and accessories such as headsets, speaker mics, and holsters. Make a list of who needs what on set and approve that list with the Production Manager before contacting walkie-talkie suppliers. When negotiating the account, often you will be able to get an extra walkie-talkie or two rent-free to cover yourself for inevitable equipment breakdowns. Maintain excellent records of who has which walkie-talkie equipment (including serial numbers), so that none are lost by the end of production. Walkie-talkie equipment is very expensive and very portable. Know the replacement value.

PAGER ACCOUNT

The crew will have various preferences from the three types of pagers available. Approve your list with the Production Manager after you get the requests in:

Numeric. These are the least expensive, but note that generally you need a Touch-Tone telephone to leave a message. Only telephone numbers can be left as messages.

Voice. Still inexpensive, these pagers do not need a Touch–Tone telephone to leave a message, but voice messages are often fuzzy. Very loud, these pagers are never used on set.

Alpha-Numeric. This is expensive. A monitoring station turns your voice message into a brief written message and sends it to the pager. Often the messages are cryptic because the spelling is very poor and possibly phonetic.

CELLULAR PHONE ACCOUNT

Note that people who use cellular phones tend not to know how much airtime costs. Since cellular phone companies have after-hours and weekend rates, take advantage of them.

TRAVEL AGENT

This is one of your best friends. Producers, Guest Stars, and Directors are very busy people who usually change their travel plans at least 100 times before boarding an aircraft. Booking the cheapest flight is rarely the way to go with all the restrictions that are attached. Make your travel agent work for you, and obtain a home number if you can.

LIMOUSINE ACCOUNT

Either you or the travel agent can arrange for limousines. Since spelling of names and specific directions can become muddled when several people are involved in the chain of communication, arranging for limousines yourself is the best way to go to ensure accuracy. It is also wise to have the name of a limousine company in any other city that you deal with repeatedly.

HOTEL ACCOUNT

Tour hotel rooms in early pre-production. See their facilities. As production nears, you will not have the time to do so. Take your camera and take pictures like a location scout. You will find it easier to talk about the hotel to a visiting guest when you have actually been there and have photographs to remind you and to show the guests.

RESEARCH COMPANY

Check with the Production Manager if you will be clearing the script for legal purposes, then find a company best able to serve you. Clearance companies read the script and note potential trademark infringements, for example. You will find names of companies in your reference books. (More about clearances is in Chapter 20: "It's Clear to Me Now.")

CUSTOMS BROKER

This is one more of your best friends, helping you to bring all sorts of items across the border. Find one and prepare a letter giving him power of authority to clear packages through customs for you. Obtain a home number if you can. (More about customs is in Chapter 19: "Crossing the Border.")

CREDIT CARD NUMBER

The Production Manager may furnish you with the company's credit card number for use with discretion in emergencies when only a credit card will get the job done. Keep this number well protected.

C. YOUR REFERENCE BOOKS

Part of the kit you bring to a production is your set of reference books. I will not mention this book, because you obviously already have it. Over time, you will collect a wealth of reference paperwork (such as contact and crew lists) from every film you complete. The more extensive your collection, the more the crew will refer to your library as much as you will.

THE REFERENCE BOOKS CHECKLIST

- ☐ Telephone Book (White Pages & Yellow Pages)
- ☐ City/Area Film Reference Book
- ☐ Other City Film Reference Book
- ☐ More Reference Books
- ☐ Who's Who Books
- ☐ Binder of Contacts

☐ Zip Code/Postal Code Book
☐ Map Book of The City
☐ Union Information (Crew)
☐ Union Information (Cast)

TELEPHONE BOOK (WHITE PAGES & YELLOW PAGES)

This is your first and foremost research tool. Never underestimate its value in helping you find something or someone.

CITY/AREA FILM REFERENCE BOOKS

Your local bookstore (that sells film books) will have reference guides to your local area. In Los Angeles you can use the BluBook; in New York, the Madison Avenue Handbook; in Toronto, the Focus Toronto; or in Vancouver, Reel West Digest. The list goes on. Government Liaison Offices also have publications for your reference library. All these guides are valuable in that they categorize companies and individuals in film-related sections.

OTHER CITY FILM REFERENCE BOOKS

If you are dealing with another city repeatedly, you would do well to buy the guide to that area too. From these books you can find, for example, that limousine company or costume shop you need.

MORE REFERENCE BOOKS

Your local bookstore or your local Government Film Liaison Office will have a wealth of other reference books. How much you want to spend will be the deciding factor on how many books is enough.

WHO'S WHO BOOKS

Although optional, Who's Who books regarding the film industry are very handy for Producers and Directors when casting, and when they cannot obtain the guest star's list of credits from the agent or manager fast enough.

BINDER OF CONTACTS

Your list of contacts will grow as your experience grows. Keep a binder of past crew lists, cast lists, and contact lists.

ZIP CODE/POSTAL CODE BOOK

Companies can order this from the post office.

MAP BOOK OF THE CITY

Have detailed maps or map books of the city and area both for the Office Production Assistant and for the office. You will be making location maps when the Locations Department cannot.

UNION INFORMATION (CREW)

All unions and guilds (from technical to directors to writers) have agreements and membership lists worth acquiring. The Production Manager will refer to these lists when looking for crew, and you will refer to them when looking for daily crew, and to complete the crew contracts (known as "deal memos").

UNION INFORMATION (CAST)

Actor's unions have agreements and forms you will need in completing cast contracts. Their membership list is in the form of a book or series of books that depict actors by photograph. These books are extraordinarily useful to Producers and Directors for casting. (More about cast contracts is in Chapter 13: "Everyone'sA Star.")

* * *

As a house becomes a home, these empty rooms are becoming a production office. With your homemade office nearby for frequent reference, you have just completed the "big" set-up. Be proud. In essence, you have a production office ready to function, and you are only in Chapter 2! Over time, you will find that each office has slightly different needs; not all offices will require a full set-up from bare floors and walls. Revise this chapter to suit each production's needs and your own personal style of production coordinating as it develops. But now is the time to add people to the office and stir.

LOST AND FOUND

When the Office P.A. calls in sick, you have to hire a Daily P.A. very quickly. There is no time to review qualifications or check references. In such an instance I hired a fellow who had been begging me for his chance to "break into the film industry." And as with many such P.A.s, I'm sure he embellished his own merits in order to get the job. Embellishing is okay, but lying is a bad career move. He said he was a very experienced driver and knew the city well.

Run #1: First up in the day, I sent him to our payroll company to drop off the payroll. The company was right downtown. The trip normally takes 15 minutes from the office in the east end to get there and 15 minutes back. We didn't hear from the Daily P.A. for over 4 hours. He never called. He never wrote. I was confused, then concerned, then worried. The P.M. needed him for another important run and I had to send the Production Secretary in the P.A.'s absence.

When he finally called, he was at a telephone booth in an industrial area of the west end. He was lost. Didn't have a map. Didn't know the city at all. Didn't know that downtown was a small collection of very tall office buildings, and when he wasn't driving in that vicinity, he wasn't downtown. I directed him back downtown and asked him to buy a map en route. He returned to the office — run completed — another 3 hours later. That was 7 hours for a 30-minute run. I hoped he was just having a bad day and would schedule the next run for him closer to the office.

Run #2: I asked him to pick up some stamps at the drugstore one block away from the office. He borrowed the Production Manager's car and took 45 minutes to get there and back. He could have walked faster. Another important run came up in his absence. It had to be delayed. Upon the P.A.'s return, he broke the key in the ignition thereby making the P.M.'s car undrivable. He finally admitted that his driver's license was considerably newer than he had originally let on and that he didn't know the city at all. At this point, the P.M. asked me to send him home.

We've never seen him since. We just hope he got home all right.

YOU AS A BOSS

Hiring and Managing Office Staff

The roles are now reversed. You are sitting in the chair across from the seat you occupied a mere few days ago. You are about to hire your first assistant. You are not sure you know how to hire and manage a staff. You are not sure how to be a good boss. On some films you will be the Coordinator, Secretary, Production Assistant, and Receptionist. On other films you will have the luxury, or the necessity, of having people report to you in these positions. It may seem daunting to have the responsibility of hiring, managing, and sometimes even firing people, but it is not as difficult as it first appears.

A. WHO YOU ARE LOOKING FOR

Most everyone wants to work in the film industry. However, many of the new-to-the-film-industry applicants will want that mythical creative job with great pay and lots of responsibility because they think the work is easy and the pay is enormous. These are not the people you want as your assistants. You need team players, not self-imagined leaders. On a crew of 10 people, it is true that each person has great responsibility and a varied set of tasks to do. That is the beauty (and the nightmare) of low budget. On a crew of 50 or 75, the same set of tasks has to be divided between many people, and on individual analysis, each person's job may seem small and pointless. You need people who can see themselves as an integral part of the whole picture, because that is what they are.

B. THE PRODUCTION SECRETARY

The Production Secretary is your right hand. You will be spending a lot of time with this person, trusting him/her with many responsibilities, and asking him/her to do a lot for you. Where this is a union position, check with union lists for available Secretaries. Where this is a nonunion position, you can get names from government liaison offices, film clubs or organizations, and word of mouth.

1. Telephone "Interview"
Before committing to an interview time and date, find out if the potential Secretary is pleasant on the telephone, and ask each: (1) are you available for the term; and (2) how proficient are you on our computer system/programs.

2. Research Before the Interview
Even if the credentials are incredible, call to check with former employers. The resume may seem impressive, but this person may have been fired from all those fabulous previous jobs.

3. Conducting the Interview
Here are a list of questions you will need to get answered either directly or indirectly during the course of the interview:

a. Do you enjoy answering the telephone?
You will be surprised how many hate answering the telephone and will tell you so.

b. How familiar are you with production paperwork like production reports, call sheets, etc.?
If experience is limited, ask yourself how much time you have to teach this person, and how quickly might he/she learn.

c. How do you deal with stress? With difficult people?
This is a difficult question to answer, but worth discussing.

d. How organized are you?
This is critical for filing, and for tracking the distribution of the reams of paperwork that you will do.

e. How do you deal with boredom?

This industry has always been a "hurry-up-and-wait" industry.

f. Can you write legible phone messages?

Check out their handwriting quality.

g. How proficient are you with the computer system?

If you can test the person, do. Some will say they are experts, but will have endless difficulty turning on the machine when it is in front of them. If testing is impossible, discuss the features you need this person to use on the computer, like an oral test.

h. What is your ambition?

Discover if this person is planning to leave in a few weeks when a higher paying job comes along.

i. How do you feel about long hours?

Determine if this person thinks a long day is 8 or 18 hours.

j. How much money do you expect to make?

Determine if this person has goals higher than the budget can allow.

Take your own mental notes during the interview. Learn about this person's manner, attitude, honesty, and maturity. Can you work with this person? Will he/she put forth the type of professional image you want?

4. After the Interview

Make written notes about each person after the interview and review them later. Discuss the applicants with the Production Manager before making your decision.

5. How to Delegate to the Secretary

Now you have hired the Secretary of your choice. How to delegate work to this person is rather hazy and very personal. Basically, know that you are responsible for everything that happens in the office (ie: in this book) and you can divide the tasks as you see fit. Here are a few ideas on specific responsibilities often delegated to the Secretary:

Telephone Reception. When the telephone gets too crazy, the Office P.A. and the Coordinator can help out.

Paper Distribution. The Coordinator with the Production Manager makes up the list of who gets what, but the Secretary carries it out and monitors it.

Shipping & Receiving. The Coordinator assists with custom requirements depending on who has more experience in that area.

Organize P.A. Runs. Sometimes the Coordinator assigns the runs to the Office P.A., sometimes the Secretary does.

But no matter what the Secretary does, he/she should constantly report to the Coordinator what jobs are in process, so that the Coordinator can be informed, aware, and be able to put those jobs into priority.

C. THE ASSISTANT PRODUCTION COORDINATOR

When there are two assistants to the Coordinator, the main assistant is the Assistant Production Coordinator, the second assistant is the Production Secretary. In some cases, people are tending away from any titles that include "Secretary" and moving toward titles that include "Assistant." When there is one main assistant who is inexperienced, it is wise to call that person a Production Secretary, leaving the Assistant Production Coordinator title for

31

an experienced person. This scenario gives your assistant room to grow within the position, and therefore receive recognition for that growth.

D. THE OFFICE PRODUCTION ASSISTANT

You will probably hire plenty more Office P.A.s than Secretaries in your time. The reason for this is that the Office P.A. position is the entry level job that everyone who wants to break into the film business covets. Unfortunately, once achieved, many are disillusioned when they discover the job is not a creative position after all. They take orders all day long, drive around the city like a courier, make coffee, and learn how to remove paper jams from the photocopier. At this point they get bored, feel unimportant in the making of the film, lose interest, and do the job badly. Here are some tips to narrow the search for genuine workers:

1. Cover Letters
If resumes do not have cover letters, toss them. You will learn more about a P.A. by the cover letter than by the fact that the resume says he/she delivered a newspaper at age 16. This is an entry level position, so chances are the resume will not have any "Office P.A." credits on it yet.

2. The P.A. Interview
Here is what you should determine during the interview:

Does this person have a good attitude toward working long demanding hours?

Does this person have some idea about what an Office P.A. does?

Does this person seem intelligent with a good memory?

Is this someone who will enjoy the job, not grow bored in two weeks?

Is this someone who can drive the type of production car you have?

The requirements may not sound like much, but you will be surprised who is out there hoping to break into the film industry. You will interview P.A.s who think they deserve your wage per week, P.A.s who think they have to be hired because they know someone on the show, P.A.s who are ready to start their own production company, but who want to make a quick buck before doing so, and even P.A.s who think answering phones, making coffee, and fixing the photocopier is beneath them. Remember: attitude, attitude, attitude, then choose accordingly.

3. How To Delegate To The Office P.A.
Here are things that you should insist upon:

The P.A. should write everything down. First things first: make sure the Office P.A. has a notebook and pen at all times. You will give this person lists and lists of things to do, and each task may sound simple, but the sheer number of them dictates that something will be forgotten if not written down.

The P.A. should keep in constant contact with the Coordinator. Ensure that the Office P.A. has a pager at all times, or make sure he/she calls you from every location traveled to in case there is a change in plans for the office runs. An Office P.A. out of touch for hours at a time is a dangerous gamble that nothing will change in his/her absence in this very "immediate" business.

Double-check that the P.A. did the tasks. Take nothing for granted. Give the Office P.A. a task and explain why it has to be done in a certain way, get them to tell it back to you so that you know they understand. In time, such double-checking may not be necessary, but at the beginning of a show, it helps to teach the P.A. how things are done and why. If you tell half a tale, expect half a job.

Check the detail of the P.A.'s paperwork. Teach the Office P.A. about purchase orders and petty cash reports. Teach them detail.

The P.A. should know who to report to/take orders from. The Office P.A. takes orders primarily from the Coordinator. Do not let the P.A. do runs for any other crew member, including the Producers and Production Manager, without talking to you first. The Coordinator is responsible for the priority of the P.A.'s runs. That also means that sometimes the P.A. must sit waiting in the office until the next task is ready. But that is the true nature of film — hurry up, then wait.

The P.A. should have things to do when waiting. Give the P.A. some responsibilities. This way you can learn if he/she is indeed responsible or not. Put the P.A. in charge of the weekly photocopier paper count (so you never run out of any color), monitor the Polaroid film stock, fax supplies, coffee and water supplies, check the status of the distribution table, and so on. He/she can make more coffee during a "wait" period, help with answering busy telephones, or ask the Secretary and Accountant if they need help. Get him/her to report back to you on these responsibilities. If all else fails, there are still plenty of learning opportunities for the P.A. who wants to succeed, like learning how to read a production board over reading the daily newspaper.

The P.A. should know what runs happen on a regular basis. The responsible P.A. can anticipate runs that happen on a regular basis, and help you manage his/her time; for example, delivery and pick up of the payroll for Accounting, weekly runs to the companies that have wall envelopes, petty cash runs, cast contract runs, script package runs, grocery runs for office craft service, and lunch runs for office people too busy to leave the office.

4. The Best Office P.A. In The World
Since many P.A.s dream about that mythical creative job, you can dream about that mythical perfect Office P.A.:

Always has a map book of the city. Knows the nearest liquor store, beer store, and post office and their hours of operation. Knows how to fix a jammed photocopier and fax machine. Knows how to use the telephone, fax machine, photocopier, coffee and water machines. Makes coffee first thing in the morning and when the coffee is low. Buys a few snacks for the office as allowed by petty cash and the Production Manager and Coordinator. Never lets the car run out of gas or windshield washer fluid, especially if borrowing the car from another crew member. Never lets petty cash run too low. Never leaves the building or room without letting the Coordinator know where he/she is going and for how long. Anticipates what runs happen on a regular basis. Knows how to open the office by self or close it (for example, on a weekend). Treats original scripts with great respect so that the paper will not be mangled by the photocopier. Always looks for something to do to help pass the time, and besides, there always is something to do. And finally, knows how to tell a good joke!

E. THE CRAFT SERVICE PERSON

Though the Craft Service Person works on set making food available to the crew and cast between meals, the Coordinator can be the one to hire this person. Where does the term "craft service" originate? I have no idea. Just think "food." Craft Service is often a nonunion position, and it is another entry-level position — the only true entry-level position that gets to work on set. If attitude is key in hiring the Office P.A., it is doubly so in hiring the Craft Service Person.

1. Interview Discussion
During the interview, discuss the following:

The work hours are long. Coffee must be hot and ready on set 15 minutes prior to the first pre–call. That means the Craft Service Person is on set about a half hour before call time, and it also means he/she is the person on set with some of the longest hours.

It is an entry-level position. If the job gets paid a flat rate, tell this person not to work out the hourly wage. You can tell him/her right now, as an entry-level position on set, Craft Service is paid the least and works the most hours of any crew member. It is a fact. But know that the position is excellent for observing many jobs on a working film crew and can help direct their own careers. When the Craft Service job is well done, the crew will help that person move into any department he/she wishes.

How to feed the crew. Imagine feeding fifty different people with fifty different tastes in food. No one can ever satisfy them all, so do not exhaust yourself trying. Present fresh food to the crew to renew their energy throughout the day. Serve the food in a pleasant manner. That is it. Picture how much food the number of crew will eat, double it and double it again. Crews eat a lot.

Monitor the craft service budget. It is very easy to go over budget in this department, so you need someone who can monitor a budget responsibly.

Driving abilities. The Craft Service Person needs to be able to drive a cube van (or not be afraid of driving one), unless the production budget only allows a panel van. Check with the Production Manager.

The job is responsible. If the Craft Service job is done well and professionally, you will find yourself treating this person as a department head instead of as an entry-level position. The job is as responsible as the Craft Service person wants to make it.

Need a good attitude. If someone is always wanting to do the next job up the ladder, that person will never fully enjoy the present work. When he/she moves up to the next job, there will always be another rung to look toward. Enjoy the steps along the way. This is advice for any job, including yours. The bonus of the Craft Service role is the opportunity to watch what happens on set and learn like a fly on the wall. The weight of the position is that the Craft Service person can set the mood of the set with his/her attitude, just like a morale officer.

2. Craft Service Companies
Many craft service companies save you the trouble of hiring crew for this position and possibly teaching someone from scratch. Their staff is usually prepared and knowledgeable about the job and their role on set. You can still discuss the above concerns with the company about the person they will hire for you. Make sure you meet and introduce yourself to this person.

F. FIRING STAFF

Sometimes you will have to fire someone for poor job performance. There is nothing easy about doing so. Imagine that someone falling down on his/her knees and begging for you not to fire him/her. Imagine firing someone and not realizing it is his/her birthday tomorrow. If you think it has to be done, consider the following:

a. Weigh the pros and cons

Film production contracts are basically short and you have very little time to teach someone the job he/she has been hired to do. Have you given this person the chance to improve? Have you talked to him/her about the seriousness of the situation? If so and there is no change, you cannot keep covering for this person.

b. Decide without emotional involvement

Never fire someone out of an emotional reaction, like anger or frustration. Cool off and decide logically if firing is the right solution. Talk this situation over with the Production Manager.

c. Is there enough time to hire someone new?

If there is only a week or two until the end of the production, firing the person may not be worthwhile. Teaching someone to fill-in for the final two weeks may be more work than putting up with a poor worker. This is the reason you should always check with previous employers when hiring someone.

d. How to fire someone

After all your consideration, if the decision is to fire the person, offer an explanation for your decision. It is not easy, but know that you have done all you can. If your reason is valid, the next person you hire will excel at the job, and the person fired will go on to excel in another job.

* * *

You are a manager of a staff now. You are the leader of the office team. Use the position wisely. Give your staff positive feedback, too. Do not make a habit of private talks only being critical. Managing staff will always have its ups and downs, since both managers and staff are human, after all. You will all make mistakes. Just realize that your assistant today may be your boss tomorrow. Together you must create a team to prepare for production now.

Hot Copies

Yes, a photocopier does have a mind of its own. It is only trying to be an artist when it jams and folds fifty sheets of paper into tiny little accordions in the duplexer. It wants to be fed when it runs out of paper or toner. And its favorite pastime will always be complaining about the weather by feeding multiple sheets of paper through at the same time. But understanding the mind of the photocopier will build a mutually beneficial relationship.

The Production Manager decided that no production office needs air conditioning in the summer. Summer is too short. Even heatwaves last only a few days. All he had to do was put up with the office staff's complaining and all would be well sooner than later.

Heatwave day #1: The office temperature started in the morning at 115 degrees Fahrenheit. The air was thick with humidity. Even a sauna would have been more refreshing. People moved slowly, and the photocopier decided that enough was enough and stopped working. It refused to feed any less than five humid-stuck–together sheets of paper at any one time. No production information could be copied to anyone on the crew. No scripts. No schedules. No deal memos. We went home early.

Heatwave day #2: 113 degrees. We bought and rented fans to cool off the copier. It appreciated our attention and copied about three sheets of paper before shutting down. Tempers quickened. Work pace slowed. No information got to the crew this day either.

Heatwave day #3: 115 degrees. A balmy 110 outside. We tried to trade in the photocopier for a more hardy machine, but no copier would submit itself to this working environment. Added more fans. Kept holding on to tempers. How long can humans or machines put up with this heat? Five copies today. Not even a dent in a full script.

Heatwave day #4: P.M. arranges for air conditioning. Copier is happy and starts to work again. Coordinator decides that a photocopier has the power to save lives.

COUNTDOWN TO PRODUCTION

Checklists for Pre-Production

You have an office. You have a crew. You are in pre-production. Go. This chapter will help you to do just that. In pre-production, the pace of work seems easy and relaxed in each department, but as the first day of principal photography nears, stress heightens and nerves become on edge. There is nothing like a deadline to change the feel of the workplace. Rather like preparing for a wedding, use these checklists to count down to the first day of shooting.

A. THREE WEEKS OR MORE BEFORE PRODUCTION

Dress the distribution table as soon as possible with paperwork of information approved by the Production Manager for distribution. You can go through this list every day to check if you can revise, update, or complete something on it. Samples of many of these forms are in the Appendix.

- ☐ Crew List
- ☐ Cast List
- ☐ Contact List
- ☐ Crew Deal Memos
- ☐ Catering Choice
- ☐ Director Medical
- ☐ Script Research
- ☐ Script Revisions
- ☐ Shooting Schedule
- ☐ Production Schedule
- ☐ Pre-Production (Prep) Schedule
- ☐ A.D. Breakdowns

☐ Continuity Breakdowns
☐ Cast Contracts
☐ Nurse/Ambulance Attendants
☐ Cast Packages
☐ Travel for Crew/Cast
☐ Immigration
☐ Cast Medicals
☐ Insurance
☐ Customs
☐ Equipment Orders
☐ Film Stock
☐ Audio Tape Stock
☐ Polaroid Film Stock

CREW LIST

Place a crew list on the distribution table as soon as possible. On page one, list the addresses of all the production companies involved, then start the crew list itself with all the producers in order of importance. Get the Production Manager's approval.

CAST LIST

This list includes the character names, actor names, home addresses and telephone numbers, respective agent names, addresses, telephone numbers and fax numbers. Do not identify any actors on the cast list that have not been approved, or until you have a deal memo in your hand to prove they are on the film. Some actors prefer not to list their home addresses and telephone numbers. Often they will let you and the A.D.s have the information for emergency use only. Honor their wish for confidentiality.

CONTACT LIST

Once you start generating accounts, you can add this list to the distribution table.

CREW DEAL MEMOS

Have blank union and nonunion deal memo forms ready. Approve the forms with the Production Manager. The head office Legal Department may have blank forms they already prefer. Make sure crew members fill out the correct forms. Staple tax forms, corporate forms, and/or permit forms to the appropriate deal memo so that all the correct paperwork gets completed at the same time. Once signed by the crew member, each deal memo can gather in the Production Manager's file on your desk for countersignature by the Production Manager at one of your daily meetings. Keep an extra crew list as a checklist as deal memos are completed. Chase down missing deal memos and keep in touch with Accounting; the missing forms may end up there before they come to you for countersignature.

CATERING CHOICE

The Production Manager can choose the caterer from a list of choices you generate from your experience or film reference books.

DIRECTOR MEDICAL

Check with the Production Manager if the Director is to be covered on the insurance policy. If so, arrange for a medical with a doctor approved by the insurance company. Note that some Directors have a kind of illness called "Gosh–I–forgot-the-appointment-again."

SCRIPT RESEARCH

If it is in the budget, send off the script to a script research company as soon as the Producer says the draft is ready for clearing. Keep the research company informed of all script changes after that draft. It is wise to telephone first to warn them about impending changes in order to get speedy results. Art departments wait with bated breath for these reports so they can make signs with "clear" names for set.

SCRIPT REVISIONS

Trying to keep up with script revisions is like trying to hold on to a waterfall. In time, you will learn who is affected most by which change, and will be able to inform the appropriate department before the typed revision comes out. Until then, keep in touch with the Producer about the estimated arrival of the next wave of revisions, and publish the changes as fast as possible. Hand them out to each department and put them on the distribution table.

SHOOTING SCHEDULE

With more and more A.D.s using computers, the Coordinator rarely has to type up a shooting schedule, but can just copy it. The only downfall to this is that you must keep making sure that the present schedule you have is the current one. If the A.D.s do not have a computer, type up this form from their breakdown notes. Get the information onto the distribution table as soon as possible.

PRODUCTION SCHEDULE

More simple than a shooting schedule, this schedule lists the production's plan on a weekly basis. Identify which weeks are prep weeks, which are shoot weeks, which are wrap weeks, and which weeks production is on hiatus. Put all this information onto one page. It is very useful to all sorts of departments in production and at head office. Note that the term "wrap" is used to describe the end of the work day as well as the time after end of the entire shoot (when items are being returned and "wrapped up").

PRE-PRODUCTION (PREP) SCHEDULE

On a daily basis, the A.D.s will generate a list of what is going to happen tomorrow and for the rest of the week. This is the prep schedule. It is another item for typing, copying, distributing around the office, and placing on the distribution table very quickly. Confirm with the A.D.s if anyone affected by the schedule needs to be called with the information. Not everyone affected reports to the office on a daily basis yet.

A.D. BREAKDOWNS

A.D.s basically generate a lot of paperwork to get out to the crew. If it is in the script, they break it down. You distribute it to the crew.

CONTINUITY BREAKDOWNS

The Continuity Supervisor cannot come close to the A.D.s in the amount of paper generated in prep, but the day/night breakdown and script timings are memos you will need to distribute right away.

CAST CONTRACTS

The deal memos come from the Casting Director. Know the actor's union agreement before typing them up. The agreement may not be the best for late night reading, but you will find it incredibly useful before working with cast contracts. Get permits as needed. If the actor is young enough, check with the Production Manager about arrangements for a tutor.

NURSE/AMBULANCE ATTENDANTS

Check with the A.D.s if a Nurse or Ambulance Attendant is required on set for any specific days. If so, arrange one. Nurses are on set for minor stunts, and Ambulance Attendants for major ones.

CAST PACKAGES

As the cast is contracted, send the Office P.A. to each one with a "welcome aboard" package including: script, schedule, cast list, crew list, call sheet (if available), and a personalized welcome letter. Keep track of which version of each paperwork you have sent to each actor.

TRAVEL FOR CREW/CAST

For visiting performers or crew, you are a travel agent. Once one is confirmed, you will need: flights, limousines (both ends), hotel, flowers in hotel room, per diem from Accounting, script package (sent by courier), and possibly an immigration permit.

IMMIGRATION

Contact the Immigration Department early! Warn them that you are going to use a foreign performer or crew, even if you do not yet have a name. Then keep them abreast of the information as it unfolds.

CAST MEDICALS

Like the director, most lead performers are insured and need medicals. If performers live out of the city, your insurance agent can furnish you with appropriate doctors closer to where they live. The sooner these medicals are done, the sooner the performers are insured. Be speedy.

INSURANCE

Have blank accident reports in your filing cabinet. Have even the most reluctant crew fill them out for any type of accident or injury. You never know when a small accident is going to develop into a larger problem. Memory fades with time. Fill out the forms immediately. The Production Manager will let you know which reports need to be forwarded to the insurance company.

CUSTOMS

You have already appointed a broker in Chapter 2. Brokers help you move equipment, clothing, or basically anything across the borders of the world. They alone know what reams of paper need to be filled out each time. Be aware that clothing has to win the award for most difficult to cross a border, so when Wardrobe starts shipping clothing in, get as much lead time as you can for customs clearance.

EQUIPMENT ORDERS

The Production Manager will deal with the basic equipment packages, but if you are tracking the purchase orders, you will be hit for the specialty equipment orders like cranes, man lifts, and jib arms. Get all requests approved by the Production Manager.

FILM STOCK

When you know what the Camera Department needs, order the film with a purchase order. Know that they will be doing camera and film tests before first day of shooting. Also, set up a delivery schedule so that you only have to store the minimum amount of precious raw film stock in the less than ideal environment of the production office.

AUDIOTAPE STOCK

Order this for the Sound Department when you know what stock and how much. Some Sound Mixers supply this stock themselves.

POLAROID FILM STOCK

Wardrobe uses it on set and in fittings. Continuity uses it for each shot. Hair/Makeup Department uses it, too. Polaroid film is very expensive, so get a good supplier, buy it by the case, and hide the film in an office drawer so that the stock gets used, not abused.

B. Two Weeks Before Production

Review your list for three weeks before production, and address these issues:

☐ Script Research Report Is In
☐ Cast Medicals In
☐ Film Stock In
☐ Audio Tape Stock In
☐ Craft Service Order
☐ Continuity Forms
☐ Battery Stock
☐ Expendables Order
☐ Catering Deal Memo
☐ Stunt Contracts
☐ Forms for Call Sheet and Production Report Chosen
☐ Rehearsal Room
☐ Arrange Pre-Production Party

SCRIPT RESEARCH REPORT IS IN

The research report for the script should be back and distributed. Keep the research company informed of any script changes, especially any kind of character and company name changes.

CAST MEDICALS IN

Depending on casting status, this should be done, too.

FILM STOCK IN

Depending on the Camera Department, this should be in, too.

AUDIO TAPE STOCK IN

Some Sound Mixers arrange to pick this up themselves. Check to see that it has been done.

CRAFT SERVICE ORDER

If Craft Service is using any of your accounts (like coffee and water), the orders should be in with enough lead time for delivery before the first day of shooting.

CONTINUITY FORMS

Review the forms that the Continuity Supervisor is going to use. You may need to arrange for printing of NCR ("no carbon required") forms by the hundreds before shooting.

BATTERY STOCK

Get orders from the Camera and Sound Departments, then use your battery supplier.

EXPENDABLES ORDER

Grips, Electrics, Camera, and Sound will have orders. Expendables are everything from sticky tape to gels to black wrap to clothes pegs. Try to get all the orders in together. One call to your supplier is better than four. Approve the extensive request list with the Production Manager.

CATERING DEAL MEMO

When the Production Manager has struck a deal with a caterer, make sure a deal memo is done.

STUNT CONTRACTS

Check with the A.D.s when stunt performers are being used and make the contracts. These daredevils tend not to be booked through Casting Directors, so their deal memos can get forgotten.

FORMS FOR CALL SHEET and PRODUCTION REPORT CHOSEN

Choose or design a set of forms that suits both the A.D.s and the Production Manager. Once chosen, give plenty of blank forms to the A.D.s.

REHEARSAL ROOM

If extensive rehearsals are going to happen, book an appropriate room.

ARRANGE PRE-PRODUCTION PARTY

Ask the Production Manager if you are to arrange a pre-production party for the crew. If so, commit to a date, get a budget for it, and start planning it now.

C. ONE WEEK BEFORE PRODUCTION

Review your previous lists for completion, and address these items:

☐ Final Production Meeting
☐ Final Location Survey
☐ Prep Production Reports
☐ Who Is the Crew Representative?

☐ Who Is the Set Safety Representative?
☐ First Call Sheet
☐ Camera Test
☐ Crew Deal Memos Done

FINAL PRODUCTION MEETING

Usually done a few days before shooting, the final production meeting is often done on the same day as the final location survey. Set up an appropriate table or room for this meeting with plenty of chairs and coffee. Attend the meeting. Clean up afterward.

FINAL LOCATION SURVEY

Usually the Locations Department, Transportation Department, and the A.D.s take care of this. Keep in touch to ensure this is happening.

PREP PRODUCTION REPORTS

Production reports in prep are for the day of the final production meeting and location survey, and for all rehearsal days. Confirm with the Production Manager which days in prep require production reports. The A.D.s can help you to complete them.

WHO IS THE CREW REPRESENTATIVE?

The crew representative needs to be named at the bottom of each call sheet. Get the name.

WHO IS THE SET SAFETY REPRESENTATIVE?

Someone from the set crew will volunteer or be appointed as the safety representative and therefore also needs to be named at the bottom of each call sheet. Find out who it is.

FIRST CALL SHEET

In the ideal world, the first call sheet, complete with location map, will be generated in time to distribute at the final production meeting. Not so ideally, a scribbly handwritten version will be given to you a few hours after the meeting for deciphering, typing, and distributing. Work with the A.D.s to get the necessary information to all the cast and crew.

CAMERA TEST

The Camera Department tends to arrange the camera test a few days to a week before shooting. Make sure the film stock is ready. After the camera test, the Camera Department should give you a final film stock order. Make sure it arrives before shooting.

CREW DEAL MEMOS DONE

Except for the crew that starts on the first day of shooting, you should have all the deal memos completed. Let people know that a time sheet is useless without a deal memo, and chase down the stragglers.

* * *

That is it. You are really moving through pre-production now. You are almost ready for day one. On different production teams, you will find differing expectations of a Production Coordinator. No matter how much work you take on, someone will always be surprised that you take care of certain matters, and that you do not take care of others. Leave that to style. You cannot do everything for everybody. Before getting to the first day of principal photography, there are a few more issues to explore in detail. You will launch into day one soon enough.

Manners, Manners

When several telephone lines light up at the same time, I help the Production Secretary by answering a few myself. We work as a team.

One day an Office P.A. hopeful called in and I happened to answer the call. He asked some detailed questions about production before introducing himself. When I asked who was calling, he insisted that he needed to talk to the Production Manager or Producer to apply for work. I explained that as Production Coordinator, I handle all the incoming resumes and hire the Office P.A. position, since the position reports to me. I said I would be happy to talk to him more about it. He became very insistent about speaking to the P.M. or Producer, and, shall I say, got very irate about the matter, insulting me and my position very pointedly along the way. I pleasantly put him on hold, then explained the situation to the Production Secretary. She took the call.

The Office P.A. hopeful was as sweet as pie to her. He was happy to have been passed along to the person he thought was the Production Manager. Never questioning her identity, he just assumed that his ranting would get him results. She asked him to send in a resume, and he agreed to do that right away. Then she asked for his name so that she would recognize the resume when it came in.

We did.

RING, RING, RING

Telephone Etiquette

It is in your office, it is in your home, it haunts you long after production has finished. It is the telephone ring. There are many particular rings of differing telephone systems nowadays. You will be haunted for years by the ring of whatever system you intend to use. I hope it is not the same ring as your house phone!

A. CHOOSING A TELEPHONE SYSTEM

If there is a telephone system already in place when you start, you are fortunate. If not, make it one of your many first priorities. Know the features you need before you start looking.

1. How many extensions (telephone sets) will you need?

You will never have enough extensions for all the crew that will request one, especially for the last week before filming when everyone is in the office. Check over your list with the Production Manager.

2. How many telephone lines will you need?

Twenty-four extensions and three lines will not work. Also keep in mind you will need a fax line and perhaps a modem line or two at the same time.

3. What features do you need and how easy are they to use?

You will want the ability to do conference calling without calling the conference operator; the ability to restrict long distance and directory assistance on some extensions; and some sets to be speaker phones. Do you want direct dialing to extensions and/or voice mail?

List your requirements and get delivery as soon as humanly possible.

B. RECEPTION: THE JOB

Reception has got to be the most underrated job on a film production. Good receptionists know who wants their calls screened and who wants certain calls to interrupt any meeting. They recognize people's voices, are pleasant and professional, and they do not lose their cool when eight lines light up at the same time. They never volunteer information to any unnamed person who calls, and on and on. They basically have a mature attitude. Here are further specifics about what the person who answers the telephone should know:

1. Who will answer the telephone?
On small productions, the Coordinator is the Coordinator, the Production Secretary, and the Receptionist. On large productions you could have enough support staff to cover each job separately. Though hard to judge accurately, know that answering the telephone will likely take up about 30 to 40% of your workday.

2. "Hello, Production"
This is the best way to answer the telephone if you are working on multiple productions out of the same office, or you do not want to advertise what production is at this phone number. Other options are "Hello, Show–Name" or "Hello, Production–Company Name." Check which greeting the Production Manager or Producer prefers.

3. "Hello, Production. Hold please."
When the telephones become extraordinarily busy, you will have to put people on hold as soon as you answer. That is okay. Just get back to each one as soon as humanly possible. Imagine all the calls coming in are long distance.

4. Answer by how many rings?
Some people get angry if you cannot answer by the first or second ring. If eight lines light up at the same time, we all know that is impossible. Answer as soon as possible. With the prevalence of voice mail, callers expect you to answer within three or four rings.

5. Telephone extension map or list

You have two choices here: (1) The map. Retrieve that floor plan map you made of the office. List the people and the telephone extensions on the map, and copy (or reduce copy) the map for reference at each telephone set. Or, if you prefer lists, (2) The list. Type up a list of crew (alphabetical by first or last name) and their telephone extensions. The map often works best because with the speed that crew is hired on a production, people tend to identify others by where they are located in the office first, and by name second. Another feature of the map is speedy access to alternative extensions in the same department if you have trouble finding someone.

6. Know how to use the features of the telephone

Know how to do conference calling, last number redial, and any other useful feature. You have to read the telephone manual because the crew will not; they will come to you for lessons on how to use the telephone.

7. Do not hand out information freely

Some productions are more confidential than others. Often callers will not identify themselves but will ask questions about the production. These people could be anyone, including reporters seeking information the publicity department wants to keep secret for some reason. Do not let your staff hand out any information. Take the call. Find out who is calling. If the call seems remotely complex or sensitive, hand it over to the Production Manager.

8. Screening calls

Find out who on the crew wants their calls screened. Chances are they will be Producers, Director, Production Manager, Accounting, and Actors.

9. Taking messages — When someone cannot take the call

Generally, if someone cannot come to the telephone, do not volunteer information as to where that person is and when he/she is expected back. Sometimes you will find that certain crew members are avoiding specific phone calls until a certain time.

10. Taking messages — Spelling

This may sound basic, but get the correct spelling of the caller's name, where he/she is calling from, the phone number, the reason for the call, and note the time and date. Thoroughness is essential. Imagine getting a phonetic message with no phone number or time, like "Gerie called," and you know a Jerry, Gerry, Geraldine, and Jahri. Who do you call back?

11. Telephone manner

It is absolutely essential to be pleasant and professional every time you and your staff answers the telephone. If you do not ensure this each and every time, it will come back to you. The old saying still rings true: you only have one chance to leave a first impression. When you answer the telephone, you are representing the company.

12. To voice mail or not to voice mail

Voice mail is a terrific invention that allows Receptionists to go to the bathroom, to handle an extremely busy telephone, and to give them more time to complete the other tasks now swamping them. The negative side effect is that voice mail is impersonal. Machines cannot tell how important the call is, and so cannot interrupt someone on another call because this call is more important, cannot tell if you are calling long distance, cannot tell that it is the one person you have been trying to reach for days, cannot tell that it is the set calling and it is also the last coin in the pay phone. Consider the importance of a person as a Receptionist. Use voice mail as a tool, not a crutch.

C. HOW TO LEAVE A MESSAGE

The A.D.s have charged you with informing the crew of call times because wrap was the middle of the night and you are the first one in the office in the morning. You are responsible. You think you know how to leave a message, but do you?

1. Leave Time and Message/Ask For Confirmation
Call the heads of departments who were not on set at wrap time and all the names on the list the A.D.s left for you to call. You will likely get answering machines. Leave the following information:

☐ The time you called

☐ Why you are calling

☐ Ask them to return the call

You need to know that each person got the message. Do not assume that because the message is on the answering machine the person got the message. Machines are not perfect. People do not always check them.

2. Make A List
Make a list of the people you called, when you called them, and if you talked to them or left a message on the answering machine.

3. Keep Trying Hourly
Every hour keep trying the people you did not speak to personally. Keep calling and leaving messages and updating your list until you speak to the person. If you never do get through, your list will be proof to the A.D.s of how hard you tried to reach that person who may not show up to set on time.

* * *

Telephones are becoming more complex every day. Even with voice mail and direct extension calling, do not forget the importance of the person that answers the telephones. If you have never answered a system telephone that rings wildly every day at the same time that you are desperately trying to do your daily work, try it. You will gain a new appreciation for the brave soul who does.

Midnight Creations

An excerpt from notes from the Production Coordinator to the Production Secretary, penned during one of those late night shoots:

1. 1:28 a.m. The call sheet is done and faxed. Office P.A. is on his way to set with it.

2. 1:34 a.m. A ginger ale is opened.

3. Please call the female lead with call time change: it's now 5:30 p.m., not 3:30 p.m.

4. Office P.A. will be in at noon; I'll work on 2:00 or 2:30 p.m.

5. Office P.A. needs to return the standard picture vehicle at 2:00 p.m.

6. Only after having cleaned both vehicles. With a toothbrush.

7. Just kidding! About the toothbrush that is.

8. I'm returning your script pages used for "siding."

9. Oh, and one more thing for Office P.A. first thing: Camera is sending back the 2nd unit equipment tonight and having it put in the P.M.'s room. Please have him take it back to the equipment house first thing.

A little later...

17. A production report to distribute — really.

18. And some lovely state of the art deal memos for that "distrib thing."

19. 1:54 a.m. Heart failure. I've been all alone since the Office P.A. left. Then I heard a voice. Of course I knew that someone was trying to make their presence known, but who? It's pretty dark and scary here sometimes — the Office P.A. came back for the craft service water.

20. 1:57 a.m. Heart resumes, and I'm alone again.

SURVIVING PRODUCTION / PATZ

21. Please find out from the Location Manager, or whomever, when the Assistant L.M. is coming back to visit the office. I need something from him.

22. No, only a signature.

23. 2:36 a.m. And now what? Another ginger ale.

24. A note to the Daily 3rd Electric from the Gaffer: Please bring the other Daily Electric in with you.

25. An equipment house order and purchase order: 200amp 3-phase disconnect for today.

26. 2:57 a.m. I realized the art department copier was still on.

27. 3:03 a.m. Found the off switch.

28. 3:12 a.m. I get my second wind. Or is it the third?

29. 3:14 a.m. False alarm.

30. You might as well send the Office P.A. out to post the mail. It keeps getting forgotten.

31. 5:14 a.m. A slew of call time changes. Please call all the actors with changes in their times.

32. As for them editors: I didn't call the Post Coordinator at night and just as well. At 1 a.m. they didn't want rushes on Thursday. At 5:00 a.m. they want RUSHES AT 7:00 p.m. Let the Post Coordinator know.

33. Please note the call sheet is pink. The Location Manager and Set Decorator know. Everyone else is to find out in the morning.

34. Gotta run to take pink call sheets to set. I've only faxed pink to head office and technical union...

58

WHERE YOU REALLY WORK

Organizing Your Work Space

You are sitting at your desk. Whether you are in your own office, or working in open concept, this is your personal space. How you organize it is most certainly up to you and your own personal style. Yet, are you ready for the reams of paper that will flow onto and off your desk? Will you be able to find every single piece of paper or information with lightning speed or will it be lost? Will passing crew members be able to read actor contracts left exposed on top of one of the great many piles? What you want are tips on handling your work space before it handles you.

A. THE DESK SURFACE

The surface of your desk will look like a sea of paper. A big sea. Paper will be constantly moving to and from your desk. Not only that, but at any given time you will need to be able to find any one sheet of paper from that mess. Separate your desk surface into sections.

1. The "To Do" List

The "to do" list is not actually a section of your desk because it should be portable, but when you are at your desk, it should sit center stage. There are many styles of "to do" lists, from calendar books, to steno pads, even to scraps of paper. Choose a method that best suits you.

CALENDAR BOOK

Choose a calendar book that shows one week for every two pages. If you write small, each day will have enough space or lines to jot down the some-times fifty-odd things to do for that day. Use the margins to note important names and numbers you may want to add to your contact list. Prep the calendar, labeling the days of the shooting schedule with day number, set name, and approximate call time. During production you can correct the call times and add the wrap times. This will be a handy reference when you are completing the production reports. Always write in a pencil dark enough to read and hard enough not to smudge.

LEGAL-SIZED LINED PAD OF PAPER

Letter-sized pads of paper will not have enough lines for the number of jobs you will do in a day. Legal-sized pads are big, and hard to lose on the desk. Use one page per day, and one line per job. You will not have to write as small as you would in the calendar book, but you also cannot glance at the full week to see what is approaching. If you find one day of stress at a time is the best for you, this is your system. Date and tear off the pages that are done and file them in case you need to refer to them again.

LINED NOTEBOOK

A combination of the legal-sized pad of paper and the calendar book, a notebook works best if you want to refer back to recent days without having to dip into the filing cabinet.

STENO PAD

The portability of a steno pad cannot be matched. The drawback is that you will constantly be flipping pages back and forth as the pages are much too small to hold all your jobs for one day. You can use this to your advantage, however, because it is a fine way to look organized, but a little frantic at the same time, thereby letting the frantic crew members relate to you.

ONE POST-IT NOTE PER JOB

If you love to put Post-it notes all over your desk, the telephone, and the walls around you, this method is for you. This is a good system to make people think you are totally disorganized and totally busy. When things get done, you come across as a miracle worker. When you delegate something, just hand your assistant the note. Drawbacks are losing notes that come loose and having no record of what is completed, since you throw out the notes as the jobs get completed.

DESK CALENDAR

A blotting paper desk calendar is not recommended. The squares are too small to list even a portion of what you have to do, and it will spend most of the time on your desk covered by the reams of other paperwork that your desk supports.

TYPED NOTES

This is another method that is not recommended, but mentioned only because on my first coordinating job, I actually typed myself a list of things to do every night for the next day. Call me crazy. I have never had the time or inclination to do it again. The Production Manager from that show still shakes his head in remembrance.

GENERAL NOTES FOR ANY "TO DO" SYSTEM

Remember that you will need to refer to your list daily, and may reference it later in production. Take the advice you gave the Office Production Assistant and note down absolutely every task you need to do, no matter how simple each may seem. Imagine trying to remember fifty different things to do. Try it. Make a list of fifty small tasks. Put the list away, then try to write it out again. It cannot be done. Finally, check off each item as completed so that you will still be able to refer to what you have accomplished.

2. The "Immediate" Notes

Always carry around Post-it notes and pen for when you do not have your "to do" list handy. These are your "immediate" notes. As people ask you to do something, write it down on a note for transposing onto your "to do" list as soon as you have time. If it is a job that requires a question of someone on set, you can put it into the "set square."

3. The "Set Square"

Mark off an area on your desk near the telephone (about 6 inches by 6 inches) with any colored tape. Put all questions for the set on separate Post-it notes for when you next talk to them. The set always calls when you are in the middle of doing something else, so with this system, all the questions are immediately handy to you and you will never have to waste time humming and hahing trying to remember why you paged them in the first place.

4. The "Desk" File Folders

These files house ongoing issues that generate for themselves a lot of paper that can take over your desk if you let them. Most of that paper is confidential, so by using file folders you will never have contracts exposed on your desk for passing crew members to glimpse. The folders are labeled:

☐ Cast Contracts

☐ Crew Deal Memos

☐ Credits

☐ Script Revisions

☐ Clearances

One file folder per issue, they sit stacked to one side of the desk with all the most current information for each issue inside. More on each of these file folders will be dealt with in later chapters.

5. The "Movement" File Folders

Use a contrasting color to the "desk" file folders. These files should be placed where passing crew can access them easily. They are used to move stacks of paper to and from the people you most deal with as the Coordinator:

THE "COORDINATOR" FILE

Okay, this may be stretching the topic of movement, but this folder holds all the backup to the items listed on your "to do" list. It will become a really fat file, so paper-clip groupings together, and give each a label with a Post-it note at the top. Then lay them in the file, one grouping slightly lower than the next, so you can see most of the grouping names as soon as you open the file folder.

THE "COORDINATOR TO P.M." FILE

This file will be used and beatup the most, since you have daily meetings with the Production Manager. Put all the paper to be signed by, approved by, and discussed with the P.M. inside the file. Encourage the crew to put items in for signature so he/she can have a single signature session, instead of one for each member of the crew. Once this system is in place, the Production Manager may not want any other in-tray. Paper-clip telephone messages to the front.

THE "COORDINATOR TO PRODUCER" FILE

Like the "Coordinator to P.M." file, this file collects paperwork and telephone messages for the Producer. This one may not get as full usage as the Production Manager's, but it will probably be close.

THE "COORDINATOR TO DIRECTOR" FILE

As it sounds, this file works the same as the above crew files, but for the Director.

THE "COORDINATOR TO PERFORMER" FILE

If you have a visiting star or guest star, this is a great way to have a temporary in-tray for him/her. Do not let this file gather information until the performer comes to you. Deliver the contents. The personal treatment will be appreciated.

6. In-Trays or Boxes

Using the "movement" file folders, you will find that you do not need a traditional in-tray. By not using an in-tray, people will have to hand you every item, thereby giving you the opportunity to quickly glance at them and determine their level of priority. But there are some in-trays or boxes that you should use. Place them on or near your desk for use by you and your assistants only.

TO-BE-FILED TRAY

Dump all the paper to be filed into this tray for you or your assistants to do the actual filing when convenient. Pencil in the file name where you would like the page to go at the top right-hand corner (especially near the beginning of production) so that both you and your assistants are on the same filing track.

ORIGINAL SCRIPTS TRAY

The second tray houses the original white pages of each script revision that is current. These pages go through the photocopier many, many times, so make sure they are treated with respect so they can continue to do their job. Label each revision with a Post-it note indicating what color the revision is (even though the title page will clearly say so). The more doublechecks there are in the system, the less likely mistakes will be made.

ORIGINAL FORMS TRAY

Like the "original scripts" tray, this one houses the original white copies of all the types of paper on the distribution table (from crew lists to contact lists to schedules, and so on). Label the color of each respective item with a Post-it note, and move outdated versions immediately over to the to-be-filed tray to avoid confusion.

B. THE HIDING PLACES

If you have a desk with a section underneath that is closed in, celebrate. Under the desk is a perfect hiding spot. If you are not blessed with such a desk, the bottom drawer of a locking, lateral filing cabinet is good, too. As for items worth hiding:

VHS TAPES OF RUSHES OR FINAL SHOWS

Copies of videotapes (like final shows) will be borrowed for personal consumption, and therefore will result in inevitable loss. Copies of rushes will not disappear as fast as master copies of final shows. Even with a sign-out sheet, people forget to put down which tapes they have borrowed. By "hiding" the tapes, crew members must ask you personally to borrow such tapes. You can keep the sign-out sheet accurate. Keep magnets and videotapes away from each other.

EXTRA CREW GIFTS

Hats, T-shirts, sweatshirts, jackets. Crew members love crew gifts, and many love having more than one per person. Keep these hidden.

C. THE WALLS

You already have wall envelopes posted for crew and for companies. Add a regular wall calendar to that, displaying several months at a time. Mark down the production schedule, noting prep weeks, shoot weeks, hiatus weeks and wrap weeks. Crew will often come to look at this. So will you.

D. THE DOORS

Check with the Production Manager what kind of sign is needed for the front door. Production may want something as simple as a photocopied sheet of paper naming the production company all the way to a professionally engraved door plaque. Find out if you should list the show title along with the production company name.

Next, choose the most artistically inclined person in your department and have that person make paper door signs for all the doors in the company (every department and every door including dressing rooms). Note the company name or show name (ask the Production Manager) and the description of the room. Door signs are great for a unified look, help when you describe to someone how to find a certain room, and teach you why wardrobe needs seven different rooms for storage.

E. YOUR RELATIONSHIP TO PAPER

There is nothing like having it down on paper. Be paper-friendly. When you have an important bit of information but no one to send a memo to, then send a memo "to file." You may be teased for thoroughness, but those around you will soon learn that if you have dealt with a matter, you have completed it and recorded it. This is very comforting in such a transient way of conducting business.

Imagine that you have been looking for the owner of a certain piece of music, and you have talked to thirty different people in five different countries over three weeks — all to no avail. When the Producer asks for a report on your research, you can remember only three contacts. You are advised to continue searching. This takes up a lot of your time and production's time. Write down what you need to do, what you are doing, and what you have done. You will never know what piece of information you will need to access in the future, but you will not be sorry if you are thorough.

* * *

Even if organization is hereditary, systems can be learned. And now you have a system of dealing with the everyday information and paper flow that will cross your desk during the course of production. You are already well on your way to developing your own coordinating style.

Any Files at All

I love two-drawer lateral filing cabinets. Filing boxes are great for those low-budget we-have-to-be-portable shows, but you can't beat a solid two-drawer lateral filing cabinet to double as a TV stand, a fax machine table, or even a distribution table. And the big drawers? Well!

The Production Manager came up to one of the filing cabinets one day deciding to look for a specific file himself. Knowing that I am an organized person, he was confident he could find the file he needed without problems and wouldn't have to interrupt me on the telephone.

The first filing cabinet drawer he opened was stacked with Polaroid film and a sign-out sheet on a clipboard. The second drawer he tried housed VHS copies of all the episodes to date and a few patch cables. He paused. There were only two drawers to this filing cabinet.

When I was off the phone, he asked me, "Do you keep any files at all?" He told me which file he needed, and I produced it right away from a filing box behind my desk. He looked from the filing box to the filing cabinet one more time. Then he shook his head and took the file into his office.

CABINETS OF FILES

Setting Up a Filing System

When all the dust is settled, the sets all broken down, the crew gone home to live their lives again, your files are some of the only source material depicting what happened during the making of the film. When you set up your filing system, you are making it up for more than just yourself. Rather than waste busy production time creating new files one by one and chance making too many duplicate or similar files, you can prepare the filing cabinet early in prep.

A. SERIES FILES

For a television series or miniseries, divide the filing cabinet into four sections as follows:

1. A-Z Files
These alphabetically labeled files do not refer to any specific episode of the series. A more specific list of file names for this section is noted below.

2. Episode By Episode Files
Make a section for each episode, labeled by episode number and title. In this section, file cast lists, schedules, credits, locations, memos, and any other information specific to that episode. These file names are marked by (*) in the file list below.

3. Production Report Files
Mark this section for production reports. Each shooting day gets a separate file. In these files, put all the production report backup information, the penciled and the typed copies of the production report. Note the shooting day as well as the date on the file folder label for future reference.

4. Forms
Since you will be making numerous forms, store them in their own section.

B. FEATURE FILM FILES

Feature films or single episode productions require files simpler than the series files, in that you are to include the episode files section in the A-Z files section.

C. A-Z FILES

Use this list to start your filing cabinet. You can substitute actual names for general descriptions (i.e., "John Doe" can replace "Lead Performer") and realphabetize accordingly.

- ☐ Accounts and Credit Applications
- ☐ Actor Union or Guild
- ☐ Art Department
- ☐ Breakdowns — A.D.'s
- ☐ Breakdowns — Continuity
- ☐ Broadcaster
- ☐ * Cast
- ☐ * Cast Contracts
- ☐ Catalogues
- ☐ Catering Menus
- ☐ Clearances
- ☐ Contact List
- ☐ Correspondence
- ☐ Correspondence — Fan mail
- ☐ * Credits

☐ Courier Waybills/Account

☐ Crew List

☐ Crew Deal Memos

☐ Crew Union or Guild

☐ Customs

☐ Distributor

☐ Director

☐ Director Union or Guild

☐ Equipment — Set (i.e., cellular phones, walkie-talkies, pagers)

☐ Equipment — Office (i.e., photocopier, fax machine)

☐ Fax Top Sheets

☐ Funding Agency

☐ Immigration

☐ Insurance

☐ Insurance — Accidents

☐ Lead Performer

☐ * Locations

☐ * Memos

☐ Music

☐ Parent Production Company

☐ Post-Production

☐ Publicity

☐ Publicity — News Clippings

☐ Resumes — Crew

☐ Resumes — P.A.s

☐ Resumes — Other

☐ * Script — White Draft

☐ * Script — Pink Draft (etc.)

☐ * Schedule — Pre-production

☐ * Schedule - One-line
☐ * Schedule - Shooting
☐ * Storyboard
☐ Story Editor
☐ Studio
☐ Travel
☐ Vehicles
☐ Wardrobe Department
☐ Wrap Party
☐ Wrap — Inventory
☐ Writers

D. Production Manger's Files

You will likely set up files for the Production Manager, too. If you put the Production Secretary in charge of the office files, you can be in charge of the more confidential Production Manager files. As a starting point, go over this list with the Production Manager:

☐ Actor Union or Guild
☐ Art Department
☐ Breakdowns
☐ Broadcaster
☐ Cast
☐ Completion Guarantor
☐ Correspondence
☐ Credits
☐ Crew
☐ Crew Union or Guild
☐ Director

☐ Director Union or Guild
☐ Distributor
☐ Finance — Budget
☐ Finance — Cash Flow
☐ Finance — Cost Report
☐ Finance — Interim financing
☐ Insurance
☐ Memos
☐ Personal
☐ Post-Production
☐ Schedule (per episode)
☐ Script (per episode)
☐ Studio

Now you have cabinets of file folders waiting for the paper to fill them. It will not take long for you to do just that. You may find it useful to post a list of these file names at your desk to remind you what your options are for filing. Revise these starter lists as you develop your style of coordinating. As you do, remember to keep in mind the question "Where would I look for this information if I were searching for it?" When you can answer that question, file the information there.

Balcony Paperwork

For one low-budget show, the entire crew and cast were housed in three cottages by a lake. Breakfasts, meetings, dinners, and social time were usually held in the big cottage's living room. I had the room with a balcony that overlooked this room. On that balcony, I set up my "office." While I was completing the production paperwork, I could also participate in the meetings and social activities.

I was known for keeping up with all the paperwork in spite of the surrounding distractions and the crew got used to looking up at the balcony if they wanted to find me. Time slipped away on that picturesque balcony, and I never knew how much time I spent there until the day that the crew bombarded me with paper airplanes made from old call sheets.

I got the hint and came down for dinner.

A FORM FOR ALL

Forms, Memos, Logs, and Checklists

You dream you are in a forest. The trees are your friends. Paper is your friend. Your dream changes into a wish for a fine collection of call sheets, production reports, and all sorts of other forms that you need to complete your task as Production Coordinator. You know there is a form for every purpose, and new forms to be made constantly. Samples and blanks of many of the following forms are in the Appendices.

A. LETTERHEAD AND OFFICE FORMS

As you create each form in this chapter, store the originals in an "original forms" file so that each form remains as pristine as possible photocopy after photocopy.

- ☐ Letterhead
- ☐ Letterhead Envelopes
- ☐ Address Rubber Stamp
- ☐ Business Cards
- ☐ Big Letterhead Labels
- ☐ Memorandum Form
- ☐ Fax Top Sheet

LETTERHEAD

First up, make letterhead for the company. If the Art Department is too busy to aid you, design it yourself. Include film title, company name, address, telephone, fax, and any other appropriate numbers. Even if the Art Department does the design, have it approved by the Production Manager and Producer before printing.

LETTERHEAD ENVELOPES

If production has the money, make letterhead envelopes at the same time as letterhead. Check if Accounting needs window envelopes.

ADDRESS RUBBER STAMP

Make a rubber stamp with the company name and address. It is a functional, affordable, multipurpose labeling device that can be used to label purchase orders, or even to create very cheap letterhead envelopes. Consider the amount of mail you will be sending out, and get a self-inking stamp.

BUSINESS CARDS

Some productions get them and some prefer not to. Locations, Set Dressing, and Art Departments use them constantly. Considering how quickly productions set up, shoot, and wrap up, business cards validate the professionalism of the company. Make blank cards (i.e., not identifying any employee name) to give you the option of typing any crew name on them. This helps you avoid having hundreds of useless named cards left over midway through the show while you run out of other names.

BIG LETTERHEAD LABELS

These labels are about 3 by 5 inches. They have the letterhead information printed on them, and are great for addressing script packages, other courier packages, and for labeling videocassettes (unless you plan to make custom videocassette labels, too).

MEMORANDUM FORM

Once you have letterhead, take one piece, remove the address and contact numbers, then make a memorandum form. Include in the heading:

- Date
- To
- Cc (carbon copy to)
- From
- Subject

FAX TOP SHEET

Take another piece of letterhead to make a fax top sheet. Be sure you leave spaces large enough for people who write big. Include in the heading:

- Date
- To
- Company
- Fax Number
- From
- Number of pages including top sheet
- Notes

B. ACCOUNTING-RELATED FORMS

Often Production Accountants come with their own forms. If not, they and head office will have definite preferences about the design of forms that relate to them. Talk to them before designing the following forms:

☐ Crew Deal Memo — Union
☐ Crew Deal Memo — Nonunion
☐ Time Sheet
☐ Check Requisition
☐ Sales Tax Form
☐ Accounting Procedures Memo

SURVIVING PRODUCTION / PATZ

CREW DEAL MEMO — UNION

These forms are available from each union directly.

CREW DEAL MEMO — NONUNION

Either the Accounting or Legal Departments have a form, or specific requirements for this form. Be sure you leave enough space for the crew member and the production company to sign and date it. There will be differences between forms designed for "employee" crew versus "corporate" crew.

TIME SHEET

Flat weekly rates make for easier time sheet forms than hourly rates and their many calculations. Design a form that works for both. Always have plenty of these forms on hand for use.

CHECK REQUISITION

This is another form that Accountants use all the time, and have very specific preferences about design. Make sure there is space for the appropriate approvals necessary for the check, and contact information of the company, in case this is the only backup paperwork Accounting will ever receive for this purchase.

SALES TAX FORM

If production's purchases can be exempt from sales tax, obtain the appropriate form from the tax office, and have the Accountant or Production Manager assist you in completing it.

ACCOUNTING PROCEDURES MEMO

Some Accountants will spell out in a memo to all crew exactly how to complete a purchase order ("P.O."), check requisition, and so on. If your Accountant does not do this, find out the procedure anyway and write it down for yourself. Each Accountant has a different style, and you will be explaining that style to crew, including the office staff and daily crew, over and over again throughout production.

C. P.M.-and A.D.-RELATED FORMS

Though the use of forms overlaps many departments, the following forms are to be designed or acquired with the help of the Production Manager and Assistant Directors:

☐ Call Sheet Form
☐ Daily Production Report Form
☐ One-Line Schedule Form
☐ Shooting Schedule Form
☐ Actor's Union Forms

CALL SHEET FORM

Simply put, the call sheet tells the crew what is being filmed on the day, where set is, when everyone is to report there (their "call time"), and what the forecasted weather is. There is no one format for making a call sheet. Collect versions from past productions, get input from the Assistant Directors, and design a form of your own.

DAILY PRODUCTION REPORT FORM

At the end of every shooting day, the Production Manager and Assistant Director must report what transpired to the Executives and to Accounting. Executives are rarely on set and must keep abreast of the running of production: Is it on schedule? What scenes were shot? What is the updated timing of the entire script? What events happened? Accounting needs to know daily what was spent to keep on top of costs as they happen: How much film and audio stock were used? What hours did the cast and crew work? What daily crew was working? The A.D.s and you are in charge of completing the form daily with input from all departments; then get approvals from the First A.D. and the Production Manager before distributing it. Design this form with the Production Manager and the Assistant Director. Treat completed production reports as confidential information.

ONE-LINE SCHEDULE FORM

Now that Assistant Directors have their own computers equipped with scheduling programs, they often make one-line schedule forms themselves. If this is not the case, design a one-line schedule to show the schedule of scenes to be shot during the entire production with, naturally, one line of text per scene. Include scene number and description, cast (by number code), script day, and script page count. This is the shortest way of expressing the entire schedule to the crew. The A.D.s will give you their scene breakdown pages shuffled into shooting order to create this schedule. (More about schedules in Chapter 16, "When It All Happens.")

SHOOTING SCHEDULE FORM

This is also a form that Assistant Directors now generate themselves. If not, design a shooting schedule as an expanded version of the one-line schedule. Also include the character names, and the various set requirements of each department as indicated on each scene breakdown page. Due to the detail, it is possible this schedule will be almost as thick as the script when completed.

ACTOR'S UNION FORMS

Contact the actor's union to find out who your representative is, and obtain the following forms for the Assistant Directors to use on set, and for you to use in post-production:

• Performer Work Reports — for the A.D.s to report which hours the performers worked each day, and you to report which hours the performers worked for post-production looping.

• Performer Contracts — there are likely several versions, so get the correct one for your production.

• Extra Vouchers — like contracts for Extras and often Stand–Ins, make sure you get enough copies for production.

• Permit Forms — for nonunion actors.

• Union Agreement — have several copies of the agreement for your reference when typing contracts, the P.M.'s and the A.D.'s.

D. Memos To All Concerned

Most paperwork you do is approved by the Production Manager and is, in essence, from the Production Manager. Here are some things to generate yourself:

☐ Color Revision Order Memo
☐ Episode List and Synopses

COLOR REVISION ORDER MEMO

As the script is revised, you will copy the new pages on another color for clarity and speed of recognition. Make a memo to "all concerned" what the colored paper order is of the script revisions. Know that some head offices have preferences. Here is a suggested order:

- White
- Pink
- Blue
- Green
- Yellow
- Any other pastel-colored paper of your choice, until
- White again, etc.

Remember that non-pastel-colored paper does not photocopy well, and you need the ability to photocopy pages over and over again.

EPISODE LIST and SYNOPSES

After working on several episodes of a series, it is difficult for anyone, writers included, to remember all the episode numbers, names, and stories. Make a list of the episodes noting episode number, title, former titles, and a one– or two–line synopsis for each. You will be surprised how useful this list is to the entire crew, to publicity, and to head office.

E. SIGN-OUT FORMS

Track all equipment rented or even exchanged when broken. Many people during the course of production will handle a lot of equipment, and it is very easy to misplace an expensive piece or two if you do not know who had the equipment last. You are responsible to return what you rented.

☐ Walkie-Talkies Sign-Out Form
☐ Pager List
☐ Keys Sign-Out Form
☐ Scripts (by label)

WALKIE-TALKIES SIGN-OUT FORM

Walkie-talkies are essential on set, very expensive, and very portable. Track serial numbers and each accessory alongside each crew name. The Assistant Directors are primarily responsible to do this on set, but a double-check tracking system in the office is also wise. When you rent a large number of walkie-talkies, you should expect a large number of parts constantly being exchanged for repair. Know where all the pieces are at all times.

PAGER LIST

Pagers are not quite as expensive as walkie-talkies, and do not break down as quickly, but you should track them nonetheless. Make a memo to "all concerned" noting crew names, pager numbers, and serial numbers. This single sheet is handy reference during production for identifying a found but unlabeled pager, and for collecting the equipment during wrap.

KEYS SIGN-OUT FORM

Either use a crew list to note the keys each person receives beside their name, or make a simple log form for people to sign out copies of keys. Using a crew list, you have to transpose all the information each time the crew list gets updated, but is an easy reference by department of who has access to the office. The act of using a sign-out form hopefully makes crew realize that there are a select number of keys, and therefore they will try not to lose them. Either way, label each key copy with indelible ink for future identification.

SCRIPTS (BY LABEL)

Though scripts do not fall under the heading of "equipment," signing out scripts is a terrific way of cutting down on excessive photocopying of the long document, and thereby saving a few trees. Put each crew member's name on file folder labels for marking each script. One sticker, one script. When crew sees that the scripts are specifically named, they will realize that the copies are limited in number, and will likely take better care of the one given to them. Discuss the names for this list with the Assistant Directors.

F. LOG FORMS

The following logs will report on where money is currently being spent, so keep Accounting updated with the following information.

- ☐ P.O. Log (Purchase Order Log)
- ☐ Equipment Rental Log
- ☐ Courier Log
- ☐ Long Distance Log
- ☐ Photocopy Log
- ☐ Polaroid Film Log

P.O. LOG (PURCHASE ORDER LOG)

If you keep no other log, keep a log of every purchase order you handle. A purchase order is a promise to pay for the item ordered. Blank purchase orders are like blank checks. With enough detail, your P.O. log can assist you listing everything that has been rented when it comes time to do the returns during wrap. Include the following columns:

- Purchase Order Number
- To Whom
- For What
- Episode Number
- Department
- Date
- Price

EQUIPMENT RENTAL LOG

If you keep a detailed P.O. log, you will not need this log. If not, note the following each time production rents an item, whether on a daily basis, or for the length of production:

- Date
- Rental Company
- Equipment
- Rental Start/End Dates
- Episode Number
- Department Ordered By
- Price

COURIER LOG

If you have an efficient Office Production Assistant, you find you will not need to courier packages around town very often. When you do courier packages, track them. You may need proof an item was sent to someone. The person in charge of shipping and receiving should be in charge of this log. Fill out detailed waybills, or keep a separate log including the following information:

- Date
- To Whom

- What Sent
- Courier Company
- Waybill Number

LONG DISTANCE LOG

Though it is nearly impossible to track all long distance charges, make a miniature log form to attach to each telephone set. Encourage the crew to complete it, especially when making personal calls.

- Date
- Phone Number
- Your Name
- Personal/Business

PHOTOCOPY LOG

If you have several companies using the same photocopy machine, have a log by the photocopy machine with pen attached to fill out each time the machine is used.

- Date
- Company or Film Title
- Department
- Number of Copies

POLAROID FILM LOG

Have a log, with pen attached, by the Polaroid film stock to track who is using which film stock and how often. Reviewing this log will be invaluable for you to anticipate how much more film is needed to complete the last few weeks or days of production.

- Date
- 600/Spectra Taken
- Department

G. WEEKLY CHECKLISTS

As the variety of supplies are used, few people will tell you it is time to order more until the shelf is absolutely empty. Check supplies on a weekly basis. Give the Office Production Assistant the opportunity to show you if he/she can be responsible by taking charge of the weekly checks, keeping track of that information, and reporting the results to you regularly.

- ☐ Craft Service Supplies
- ☐ Coffee Supplies
- ☐ Water Supplies
- ☐ Photocopy Supplies
- ☐ Photocopy Count
- ☐ Fax Supplies
- ☐ Office Stationery Supplies
- ☐ Polaroid Film Supplies
- ☐ Cleaning/Paper Supplies

CRAFT SERVICE SUPPLIES

If Craft Service is ordering coffee and water through the office supplier, talk to set weekly about Craft Service's supply needs.

COFFEE SUPPLIES

Check supplies a day before the coffee company is scheduled to call you for an order.

WATER SUPPLIES

Like the coffee supplies, check before the company calls you for an order, or before the company's automatic delivery. Water companies tend to put all companies on an automatic delivery. Beware if you have a one-time order of twenty-seven bottles; the water company may automatically send you twenty-seven bottles every two weeks until you tell them otherwise.

PHOTOCOPY SUPPLIES

Keeping in mind which colored revision is due next, check the amount of colored paper and toner you have.

PHOTOCOPY COUNT

When checking the paper supplies, jot down the number of copies used to date on the machine. You will need this number for your photocopy service agreement, for Accounting, and if you have several companies using the same machine. It is also enlightening to discover how many thousands of copies you actually do on a weekly basis. Have an office lottery, if you like.

FAX SUPPLIES

Check fax paper supplies and toner.

OFFICE STATIONERY SUPPLIES

Have an order form hanging to the office supply cabinet with a pen attached to it. Check the general supplies, like pens, on a regular basis also.

POLAROID FILM SUPPLIES

Even though you have a log form to sign out Polaroid film, crew may not tell you that they just took the last box of film. Check weekly.

CLEANING/PAPER SUPPLIES

Does the office have enough paper towels, cleaners, bathroom tissue, first aid supplies?

H. Where To Place All The Paperwork

You have a distribution table, wall envelopes, and your desk drawer. Here is a recap of the forms mentioned in this and earlier chapters, and where to put them for appropriate access.

WHAT'S ON THE DISTRIBUTION TABLE

- Script and Script Revisions
- Crew List
- Cast List
- Pager List
- Contact List
- Telephone Extension List
- Episode List and Synopses
- Schedules (all kinds)
- A.D. Breakdowns
- Accounting Procedures Memo
- Color Revision Order Memo

WHAT'S IN THE "FORMS" WALL ENVELOPES

- Letterhead
- Fax Top Sheets
- Memorandum Forms
- Check Requisitions
- Exemption from Sales Tax Forms/Proof
- Time Sheets

WHAT'S IN YOUR DESK DRAWER

- Everything else

I. INVENTORY LIST

Start making an inventory list as you acquire items during pre-produc-tion. The chance of you remembering everything that was rented or pur-chased throughout the entire film after the fact is slim. You already have a file in the cabinet labeled "wrap," so use it. The work you do now will save you hours of searching after the film is done and any crew that could help you has gone home. If your P.O. log is very detailed, it can double as your inventory list.

You now have lists to jog your memory about what is going to happen, forms to take care of all that is, and logs to keep track of all that was. Store these forms for future use. Assemble more from every production you know. Create your own collection and preferences. You are ready to anticipate, analyse, and organize. You are ready to record it all on paper.

THE LOCKED ROOM

There was a time when fax machines were considered such valued equipment that they were stored in locked rooms. This is a locked room story.

Script revisions came in from Los Angeles about 8:00 p.m. the night before each voice recording session. These changes had to be incorporated into the script, and the incorporation process was a lengthy one. Now, 8:00 p.m. Los Angeles time is 11:00 p.m. Toronto time. Since waiting until 11:00 p.m. in the office for one fax was rather silly, my co-worker and I would go out for dinner preceding this regular event.

One night we returned to the office to find the room to the fax machine closed and locked. Not good. We had about 10 minutes to figure out how to get in. Finding someone's home number who might have a key was not an option so late at night. The fax bell rang. We were out of time. Then we noticed the air vent.

There was an air vent in the general neighborhood of the fax machine in the room next door. It was our answer. We had to work fast. So, with a yardstick decked out with sticky tape on one end, my co-worker climbed onto a desk, then onto my shoulders, so she could stuff herself through the air vent above the fax machine. One by one she snagged the pages as they came off the machine, and stuffed them back through the vent to me.

Then I with sore shoulders, and she with sore neck and arms, incorporated the changes into the script and the voice recording session proceeded the next day as planned. We commented to ourselves, "So this is the glamour of working in film?"

YOUR COMPUTER AND YOUR KIT

The Coordinator's Start-Up Kit

Now that you are toward the end of the section on pre-production, you are familiar with all the work it takes to start up an office. Every time you start up a new office, you find yourself buying over and over again all sorts of the same supplies, from the rental computer, all the way to the paper and pen to write down the first telephone message. Bring these start-up supplies and your computer equipment with you, and you will have a "kit." A kit that will enable you to get to work more quickly, and a kit that production will rent from you.

A. START-UP SUPPLIES

Here is what you will need upon first arriving at the production office. Bring this kit with you, then top it up to the same level when you finish production.

- Date stamp and pad (for date stamping the mail)
- Three–hole punch
- Stapler and staples
- Heavy duty stapler (depends on your funds; for thick scripts)
- Box of pens and pencils
- Fat permanent marker (for labeling courier packages)
- Eraser
- Electric pencil sharpener
- Manual pencil sharpener (for backup when electric one fails)
- In-trays
- Scissors

- Glue stick
- Dull clear tape (shiny clear tape gets tacky in time)
- Packing tape
- Telephone message pad ("duplicates" so you retain a record)
- Paper clips and dispenser
- Ruler
- Pad of lined paper
- Desk or wall calendar
- Manila envelopes
- Letter-sized envelopes (for before letterhead is printed)
- Some file folders (to furnish the files on your desk)
- File folder labels
- Plastic or tin box for storing copies of keys
- Extra typewriter or printer ribbon
- Some of your usual courier waybills and packaging
- Pictures and knickknacks to make you feel at home

B. COMPUTER EQUIPMENT

Rental computers are fine if you cannot afford a computer of your own; however, a computer of your own is invaluable to you and your kit. In your own computer, you can collect all sorts of information that you have gathered from production to production. This information will always be at your fingertips. Your growing familiarity with one machine will also allow you to become expert at its use. Being aware that computers change and improve every few months, consider the following when deciding to purchase:

1. IBM (or Compatible) Versus Macintosh

The film industry uses both systems. If you work with one or a few companies most often, find out which computer system they use. Being computer-compatible with the parent company will save you endless retyping. Otherwise, talk to people who own both types, and try both systems out. Though software grows more sophisticated every day and several can translate documents between IBM and MacIntosh, not all programs have this ability. You are still choosing between two very separate computer systems.

2. New or Used Equipment

New computers change all the time. What was top of the line yesterday is ordinary today and is outdated tomorrow. If you can, buy the latest equipment you can afford. Used equipment may seem very affordable at the time, but too soon you may find out that you cannot upgrade your system to accommodate the latest standard software.

3. Physical Aspects of the Computer

Before purchase, try out the keyboard to make sure it is the right size for your hands. Do you like the way the mouse fits into your palm? Is the screen big enough and bright enough? Do you have to peer to look at it or hunch over? Can you find the "page up" and "page down" buttons with your eyes closed? How about the arrow keys? You are buying a computer and it will belong to you. You will use it constantly. If there is something that you find annoying about the computer when you first look at it, that something will grow to a major aggravation, guaranteed. Love your computer from the very first moment.

4. Portability

The nature of a freelance life is to work at a job for a period of time, then move home, then move to another job, then move home, then move to another job, and so on. If it takes you four trips to the car just to move your computer parts — the CPU, the monitor, the printer, and the keyboard & accessories — the frequency of your jobs should make you consider laptop computers.

5. Options and Expandability

The options available on a new computer are seemingly limitless. As computers upgrade month after month, each new option today is standard equipment tomorrow. Good features to have are a fast fax modem, the ability to add memory, the ability to add features, and long battery working time.

6. Price

As options and equipment skyrocket in quality and availability, so the prices plummet. Know that as soon as you buy a computer, a new one will be invented and yours will be marked down. Though the longer you wait, the better a computer you can buy for your money, the longer you wait, the longer you do not have a computer. Buy one at the last possible moment that you need one, then buy the best computer you can afford and close your eyes to what comes onto the market next. The computer you choose will be just fine.

7. Printer

Dot matrix printers are very affordable, but very loud and slow. Their "letter quality" typeface is satisfactory. Laser printers have extraordinary typefaces, but they are bulky to carry around and are expensive. Bubble jet (or ink jet) printers fall somewhere in between these two quality-wise and price-wise. They are often available in a portable model, too. Depending on your funds and the requirements of your typeface quality, choose the printer for you.

C. OTHER OFFICE EQUIPMENT

Not all of the following equipment is necessary to complete your kit. You decide how big a kit you would like to maintain.

TYPEWRITER

Computers have not replaced the typewriters entirely. Typewriters are still useful for typing up forms (like cast contracts), envelopes, and checks. Crew members will use one if it is placed accessible for sharing. With the onslaught of computers throughout the working world, typewriters are now cheap to buy. Have one as part of your kit.

PAPER CUTTING BOARD

After reduce-photocopying script sides, you will need to cut them. A cutting board makes this job much easier and faster than using scissors. It is not necessary for your kit, but advisable.

D. IDENTIFY AND INSURE YOUR KIT

Mark all the equipment of your kit with your name and address. A simple file folder label with your name on can be attached to almost anything in your kit for identity. This system will help you to collect all your equipment at the end of production.

As for insurance, your kit belongs to you. Get the expensive equipment properly insured.

E. COMPUTER SOFTWARE

The list of programs available to install on your computer seems endless. The choices are mind boggling. No two people or companies appear to use the same software. As first priority, buy programs that have the capability of translating to and from other programs.

Addressing all the programs available is an impossible and ever-changing task. Here is a category list of types of programs available and appropriate for you. Educate yourself about your computer. Take a course, read manuals, ask friends how — do whatever it takes to learn. Your computer is to be your right hand, and not you its slave.

1. Operating Software
IBM (and compatible) computers often operate on DOS. DOS stands for "disk operating system." Basically, DOS is a computer language that tells the

computer how to read other programs. Without it, the computer is just a series of mechanical parts. Computers are sold with DOS included.

ASCII (pronounced "askey") is the language that DOS uses to talk to the computer and to other programs. It is also known as "ASCII text" or "DOS text." ASCII can only be a series of letters, numbers, or spaces (nothing bold, underlined, or in differing fonts). It is the most basic language to which a computer can reduce a document. Because it is so basic, modems can easily send and receive ASCII text on telephone lines so that all computers (no matter what software they have) can read the file.

2. Shell or Environment Software
Microsoft Windows is the most well-known shell program. It creates a picture environment, where you can access your programs from the touch of a mouse button, instead of using a DOS command. But, Windows does not replace DOS. It makes all those icons and graphics using DOS, but just does not show you on the screen all the DOS commands it takes to create such a show. For that reason, it is called a "shell" or "environment" program.

3. Utilities Software
Both Microsoft and Norton are known for their utilities programs. Programs to unerase files you deleted by accident, or disk-fixing programs to diagnose and fix problems in your computer, are truly handy to have and know how to use.

4. Antivirus Software
This type of program is specifically made for searching for known computer viruses and fixing them. Like any regular virus, you can get a computer virus from contact with another computer, or another computer's programs or files. Antivirus software is preventative medicine and well worth it.

5. Word Processing Software
Very appropriately, word processing programs process words. You type in words, and through the program you will be able to make certain letters bold, underlined, centered, in different fonts, and so on. You can cut and paste sections of words without scissors and tape, join documents together, let the program number the pages, and perform a host of other features. Basically

this software makes your computer a very intelligent typewriter. As a Production Coordinator, this will be your most-used software. Love this program. Invest the time and money to take a course and learn how to use it thoroughly. Ask other users what they like and dislike about their word processors. Get all the features you want, and be able to use all the ones you need quickly and with little effort. Two popular word processing programs are WordPerfect and Microsoft Word.

6. Speciality Software — Script Formatting Software

Though you can format a script to look like a script on a word processing program quite fine, there is script formatting software on the market designed specifically for the film industry. Chances are, you cannot type the script in the formatting program. You need the word processor to do that. You cannot revise the script in the formatting software. You need the word processor to do that, too. What this program can do is (if you type to its formatting requirements) number your scenes (even A and B scenes), number your pages (even A and B pages), and print the script. And, if you ask, it can generate a list of characters for you. If you have the time to get familiar with this program it can be useful. Because it is software for a very specific market, courses are difficult or impossible to find, so time and experience will be your only teacher.

7. Database Software

Database programs let you input lists (like mailing lists), and reorganize those lists any way you like (even in alphabetical order by street name). Many word processors have information sorting features that make a separate database program unnecessary for you.

8. Speciality Software — Film Production Scheduling Software

This type of software is simply a database program written specifically to schedule film productions. Movie Magic Scheduling is most noted for this. The program takes the input of A.D. breakdowns of each scene, and creates a production schedule for manipulation and printing. Assistant Directors likely have this software on their computers and, as it is expensive, you may not be able to afford this right away. In any case, it is wise to familiarize yourself with this program should you have to revise the schedule in the A.D.'s absence.

9. Spreadsheet Software

Spreadsheet software is basically the blend of putting a calculator into graph paper. With the right codes in the right boxes, the program can add, subtract, multiply, divide, and average numbers for you. As you change the source numbers, the program will automatically change the totals accordingly. You can create graphs and lists with this program. Lotus 123 and Excel are popular spreadsheet programs.

10. Speciality Software — Film Budgeting Software

Movie Magic Budgeting, another known specialty program, is written specifically to aid Producers and Managers in creating budgets for film productions. Simply put, it is a specialty spreadsheet program. As a Production Coordinator, you will not need this program, but it is good to know what it is.

11. Communications Software

Communications software tells the computer how to use the modem that is attached to your machine. With it you can telephone another computer or a bulletin board service ("BBS") to send and receive information and files. There is a lot to learn about modems before you embark on using them. Talk to people who use them all the time before you start. Learn as much as you can.

12. Fax Software

Like communications software, fax software tells the computer how to use the fax feature of your fax modem. Instead of printing documents to your printer, you can telephone a fax machine and print the documents out like faxes.

13. Internet Software

To hook up to a server, provider, or on-line service, you need a collection of software that the connector will likely provide. Parts of this package include net surfing software and e-mail reading software. The Internet is terrific for international e-mail (electronic mail) and research. Though not critical at the moment, this will become more and more another tool for the Coordinator.

* * *

Congratulations! You made it through pre-production! You have a kit together that, small or extensive, gets the office up and running as soon as you walk in the door. It is time to put the pace of pre-production behind you and think about production. Cameras are rolling. The real fun is about to begin.

PRODUCTION

Grandmother on the Set

There was a day I brought my grandmother to visit the set. I don't normally bring visitors to the set, but my mother, who had been once before, was insistent that my grandmother see filmmaking firsthand. My mother, you see, sees roses in everything in life, and will always see the magic created on a film set. She wanted to share this magic with her mother.

My grandmother was predictably very silent and observant on her visit. The crew and cast were very friendly to her, and she saw a fair amount of the day's activity before going home.

Afterward she made only three comments about the day. About the crew: "Nobody bothers to dress up for work; they're all in jeans." About the time when the cameras were rolling: "Everyone seems to be standing around doing nothing." And about filmmaking in general: "I don't know how the show comes out in order; everyone looks so disorganized."

To anyone in film to whom I have mentioned these three observations, I get the same response: "How very astute of her."

WORK WITH THE ENTIRE CREW

Dealing with All Departments

You run into someone in the hallway and exchange information. You have just had a meeting. Meetings in production can be a casual, or even accidental, get-together. As the Coordinator, you will talk to everyone on the crew in order to do your job. Do this as much as possible.

A. OFFICE PEOPLE

Using the loose meaning of "meeting," here is why the Coordinator meets with people in the office.

PRODUCER

The Producer, who answers to the Executives, is responsible for the whole production, and is involved in creative decisions from casting to script. The Producer is your source of information about the casting status of Actors, and the revision status of the script.

PRODUCTION MANAGER

You are well aware by now that you and the Production Manager work hand in hand. Meet every day to get direction, gain approvals, and keep each other informed. The Production Manager is responsible for the film being made on budget, overseeing everything the Coordinator does, and anything that pertains to money.

DIRECTOR

The Director has the overall creative vision of the project, and basically gives direction to all department heads to realize it. The Director knows what script revisions and casting choices he/she wants, though the Producer must confirm these choices before you proceed. If the Director has no Personal Assistant, you will be covering such needs for him/her, too.

WRITING DEPARTMENT

There could be a Creative Producer, Story Editor, and a team of Writers. You type up and format the scripts for these people. You may have to correct their grammar. They likely want to know the page count of the typed script as soon as possible. Make sure the Producer approves each draft you get directly from them.

PRODUCTION ACCOUNTANT

Discuss with the Accountant who will track purchase orders. Arrange to complete an exemption from sales tax form. Determine how much petty cash the office will need, and who, of your team, is going to keep and monitor it.

PRODUCTION SECRETARY

As you are the right hand of the Production Manager, the Secretary is your right hand. Meet at least daily to give direction and approvals, and to keep each other informed.

OFFICE PRODUCTION ASSISTANT

As already discussed, keep a constant flow of communication going between the Office P.A. and you. This person is your left hand.

HEAD OFFICE/CO-PRODUCTION OFFICE PEOPLE

Done by telephone, conversations with these people are to determine what paperwork they need and when. Approve all requests with the Production Manager.

B. CAST AND CASTING PEOPLE

The only reason that "casting" has anything to do with "fishing" is because casting people are always fishing for the right talent to fill all the acting roles in a film.

CASTING DIRECTOR

Keep the Casting Director apprised of the latest script revision and he/she will keep you apprised of the latest status of Actors chosen. Casting Directors make the deal with the Actors' Agents, then send the deal memos to you. You turn these deal memos into cast contracts. You may also be involved in helping the Casting Director set up audition sessions, and in making and distributing audition sides to be read at the auditions.

CAST

You will be one of the first people to deal with the Actors, and therefore give them their first impression of the company. You are responsible for sending them all the paperwork necessary for them to act in the show. Keep them updated on all script revisions immediately. They are the ones that have to memorize the lines.

EXTRAS and EXTRAS CASTING DIRECTOR

Well, you do not actually have to talk with Extras (also known as Background Performers). Extras who are cast with no lines, fill the background of scenes. On film, they can pass by, walk dogs, or be crowds. Special Skills Extras (or Special Business Extras) play hockey, ride horses, and do other things on film that require a special skill. You will, however, deal with the Extras Casting Director in order to coordinate their arrival on set.

C. SET PEOPLE — ASSISTANT DIRECTORS

You deal with the Assistant Directors several times each day, funneling any information you have for set through them; therefore, they warrant having their own section. A.D.s are in charge of running the set so that the Director can be creative without worrying about the time or gathering the people and props together. That is why they seem to do an awful lot of running around.

ASSISTANT DIRECTORS

A.D.s have the lowdown on the schedule. They make it. You have the lowdown on casting status. Swap information. Inform them of special agreements in the cast contracts that affect the set (like private dressing rooms that have been promised, and drivers to pick them up daily). Decide together which call sheet form, schedule form, day-out-of-days form, and production report form to use. Find out if you have compatible computer equipment. Discuss the shoot day responsibilities in detail: Who is to call crew with the next's day call times? Who is to inform actors with change of dates? Who is to inform the crew when the call time gets pushed or pulled in the middle of the night? Before the shoot, the A.D.s will come to you to stock up on all the paperwork from the distribution table and forms from the wall envelopes for their portable office on set. Give them a hand and work as a team.

D. OTHER SET PEOPLE

Many of these people float from office to set, but their primary responsibility is to set.

LOCATIONS DEPARTMENT

These people scout and survey potential locations, then once chosen, make the location deal with the owners. Location Managers will often ask you to type up the agreement letter or contract, and arrange for insurance certificates for each location. They usually need these documents hurriedly. They will also give you location maps to attach to the call sheets. Ask for the maps early, unless you enjoy making maps at the last moment.

CONTINUITY SUPERVISOR

This person is basically the Editor's representative on set to make sure each shot will be able to cut to the next without faults, like arm movements that do not match, and burning cigarettes that change length. Continuity, therefore, makes many, many notes about and photographs each and every shot during the course of the shoot day. In prep, make sure Continuity and the Editor meet, find out what forms need to be printed, have them made, and arrange for the purchase of the correct Polaroid film for his/her camera. Also discuss the most efficient way for that paperwork to flow from set to the editing department and back to set.

TRANSPORTATION DEPARTMENT

You will see Drivers every day in the office during the course of their many runs. Talk to them often, because you can usually help them out with use of the Office Production Assistant just as they can help you out with use of a Driver.

CRAFT SERVICE

As already discussed, Craft Service supplies snack foods to the crew all day to keep them energized between meals. If this is a person you hired rather than a craft service company, this person will be new to the industry and will have lots of questions. You can help by discussing the accounts you have with coffee and water companies. Make sure Craft Service has the first–aid kit handy for the set.

CATERER

You will be calling this supplier every day with the time for lunch the next day and to let them know where, when, and for how many. Find out from the crew if there are any special needs (not requests) for catering, like food allergies.

E. DESIGN, BUILDING, AND DECORATING PEOPLE

Depending on the needs of the production, these people may have been hired before you and are already working.

ART DEPARTMENT

This department can be made up of the Production Designer, Art Director, Assistant Art Directors, and the Art Department Coordinator, or any combination thereof. They design the whole physical look of the film, especially the sets. They can make beautiful, artistic letterhead for you. They will need items messengered by you and cleared through customs. They need you to arrange for a speedy script clearance so that the names in the script are legally approved to be made into signs.

SETS DEPARTMENT

With the direction of the Production Designer, these people buy and rent the set furnishings, from lamps to furnish a house set to fake garbage to furnish an alley set. Like the Art Department, they need you for arranging couriers and customs clearances. They also need pagers from you.

PROPS DEPARTMENT

Props are anything the Actors handle as written in the script, from cigarettes to food to suitcases to clothing they carry, and so on. Props people will need your help in arranging couriers, customs, and renting pagers.

CONSTRUCTION DEPARTMENT

As the name suggests, these people build the sets for the Art Department. You do not have to deal with them much, as they are usually working before you are hired and have their own system in place of organization, but talk to them now and then to keep in touch with the progress of the production.

F. Technical People

Technical crew get hired toward the end of pre-production and report directly to set. You will have to visit set to meet them.

CAMERA DEPARTMENT

In prep, find out from the Camera Department what film stock is to be used, and order it as soon as possible. Keep informed on when the camera equipment and stock tests are scheduled, because you will likely be asked to help in those arrangements. From them, get a battery order and expendable order (like camera tape and lens tissues). Though the Director of Photography makes the decisions, it is the 2nd Assistant Camera Person to whom you will speak most often.

SOUND DEPARTMENT

The Sound Recordist (or Sound Mixer) and the Boom Operator make up this team. Find out and order what sound stock they intend to use, unless the Sound Recordist is planning to arrange for purchase of the stock. Sound always has an extensive battery order for you.

ELECTRIC DEPARTMENT

The Gaffer is the head electrician, and the Best Boy is next in charge. The rest of the team are called Electrics. These people, obviously, are in charge of the lights on the set and work closest with the Director of Photography. They will have an expendable order for you to arrange, like gels (colored-gelatin sheets or rolls to color the lights), black wrap (to mask light), and clothes pegs (to hold the gels and black wrap onto the lights).

GRIP DEPARTMENT

Also working closely with the Camera Department, Grips move all sorts of things around on the set, and create the most beautiful rigs to enable the camera to dolly around, in and through just about anything. The Key Grip is head of the department with the Best Boy Grip or Dolly Grip, second in charge. The Dolly Grip operates the dolly equipment on which the camera sits for moving shots. Get an expendable order (like tape and sash) from this team. They may also have specialty rentals they will ask you to arrange, like scaffolding and cranes. Obtain necessary approvals from the Production Manager.

G. HAIR, MAKEUP, AND WARDROBE PEOPLE

Affectionately known as the Pretty Department, these people dress and make up the actors into character for on camera.

WARDROBE DEPARTMENT

Find out which type of Polaroid film this department uses. Keep them abreast of the casting status as soon as possible, because these people never seem to get enough time to fit the cast.

HAIR/MAKEUP DEPARTMENT

These people also need to be kept informed of the casting status, but not quite so hurriedly as the Wardrobe Department.

H. SPECIAL DEPARTMENTS PEOPLE

Depending on the scale of the production, you could have any, all, or none of the following departments to create the magic of movies:

STUNTS DEPARTMENT

When the script calls for someone to walk through fire, the script calls for a stunt double. You need to know from the Stunt Coordinator who is going to play which role so that you can inform Wardrobe, and so you can whip up the appropriate stunt contracts. Also discuss the nature of the stunt with the Stunt Coordinator and the Assistant Director to determine if a Nurse or an Ambulance Attendant is required on the day. If so, book one.

SPECIAL EFFECTS DEPARTMENT

Special effects can be fires created on set, snow, rain, and so on. Often these people are from a supplier that does not work in the production office with you, so it is your job to keep them informed of meetings and script changes that affect them. Find out the nature of the effect, and how you can help. You can arrange, for example, for a representative from the fire department to be on set, or for someone to have a fire extinguisher handy. Discuss all arrangements with the Assistant Directors.

VISUAL EFFECTS DEPARTMENT

Different from set special effects, visual effects are usually computer effects or motion controlled-camera equipment (to enable computerized matching of camera movements). These people are rarely in your office full time, so keep them informed of meetings and script changes that affect them.

ANIMATION DEPARTMENT

Animation used to always be hand-drawn. More and more, it is done on computer. If you have a Visual Effects Department and an Animation Department, the first is likely creating 3–D computer effects and the second, 2–D computer effects. Whether hand-drawn or not, this is another team to keep informed of script changes and meetings that affect them.

I. Post–Production People

Post–production makes you think "after production," but it actually starts before the end. The Editor is usually aboard cutting the film together while the film is still being shot.

EDITING DEPARTMENT

There may be a Post–Production Supervisor, a Post–Production Coordinator, an Editor, and Assistant Editors. You already made sure that the Continuity Supervisor and Editor connected during pre-production to discuss the continuity paperwork. Other things to discuss with the editing team are a system for the information flow regarding the arranging for and screening of rushes, and who is to call the lab for the daily negative check.

MUSIC DEPARTMENT

You likely will not need to deal with the Music Composer very often. He/she will tend to deal with the Producer directly. If a piece of music is to be played back on set for filming, you need to arrange for this, from the transfer to appropriate format to getting the music to the Sound Recordist on set. Make sure you have an extra copy of this music in the office in case of an emergency on the shoot day.

POST–PRODUCTION LABORATORY

If you have a Post–Production Supervisor or Coordinator, you will not have to deal with the lab directly very often. You may be the one to call the lab first thing every morning for a negative check (or "neg report"). Once the film has been processed overnight, the lab will tell you if there are scratches on the negative. If there are, inform the Production Manager and Producer immediately. They will want to investigate further the severity of the problem to determine if yesterday's film will have to be reshot. Other reasons to be in touch with the lab are to arrange the screening of rushes at their facility, or to set up an A.D.R. ("Additional Dialogue Recording") session.

J. PUBLICITY PEOPLE

Though it may seem that publicity arrangements get in the way of filming, a film would have a hard time finding an audience if publicity people failed to do their job.

PUBLICITY DEPARTMENT

Be involved in arranging for the Publicity Department to visit and work on set. Keep them informed of the shooting schedule, and keep them in contact with the Producer to discuss the best days to be there. They need to arrange for interviews, for press people to visit set, for Photographers to shoot gallery shots ("posed publicity shots"), and for video teams to film behind the scenes. Keep the Assistant Directors in the loop of these conversations.

STILLS PHOTOGRAPHER

This person is likely to be on set a lot more often than the Publicity Department. Keep him/her aware of the shooting schedule, but make sure the Photographer talks with the Producer and Assistant Director about which days are expected to be most photogenic, and which are lightest in work load to allow for a gallery shoot.

K. WHEN INFORMATION IS CONFIDENTIAL

Realizing that you talk to all the departments of the production, you will often be trusted with confidential information. Some information will need to be forwarded on to others under the cloak of continued confidentiality; other information you will wish you never heard because you cannot tell anyone even though it drastically affects everyone. About confidential information, be very, very careful. When confidential information gets shared among your office staff, consider the following advice:

1. Use A Code Word or Phrase
With your Assistants, use a code word or phrase (like "you didn't really hear that") to inform them that the information they just heard, whether on purpose or by mistake, is strictly confidential, and they should not pursue the subject. Get the Assistants to respond with another phrase to let you know they understand.

2. Use Envelopes or File Folders
Never have confidential information left face up on your desk. Use sealable envelopes, or put such paperwork into file folders to hide from view, thereby quelling people's curiosity as they pass by your desk. If there is no time for using an envelope or file folder, place the document face down on the desk. Make sure the office staff understands and uses this system.

3. Be Careful When Faxing and Photocopying
Avoid faxing confidential information, if at all possible. If necessary, do not fax anything else at the same time, and do not use speed dial. A confidential fax going to the wrong recipient by attaching it to the back of another

111

fax, or by pressing the wrong button is inexcusable. When photocopying a confidential document, take the same care. Take the time to copy it on its own. Without distraction, chances are you will not leave the original in the photocopy machine. Make sure the office staff understands and abides by this system, too.

You do deal with all departments. You must earn their trust, and give trust in return. Review this chapter from time to time to remind yourself of what you can learn from each department. Talk to everyone. The constant input will be helpful and educational to you. There is always something to learn.

The Daily Chuckle

I'm proud of the fact that I have never published a call sheet without a joke on the back. It's an incentive. Crew make sure they get a call sheet at the end of the day when they know they are going to get their daily chuckle on the back. Then one day the hydro building across the street from the production office blew up.

The office power went out, and we were left with one emergency telephone in a darkened, silent office. Without a telephone system and computers, there was little to do but watch the black smoke billow out of the remains of the building across the street. Our front step afforded us a picture perfect view. The wind was blowing the smoke away from us.

The emergency crew arrived quickly and got to work breaking windows and, I suppose, drawing straws for who was to go inside. The police soon noticed us, and came over to give us 10 minutes to leave the building and area. If not, they would seal us in. Several blocks already had been closed off for the crisis. Oh boy.

We could only grab what was portable and absolutely necessary. The Production Manager took the budget, the Accountant took the crew deal memos and cost report, and the Production Secretary grabbed a selection of office supplies. I looked at my computer. It was a desktop model. Too big. I still had the call sheet to do today, so I grabbed a copy of the shooting schedule, a typewriter, and the joke file!

Later, in a makeshift space at head office, the call sheet was completed, the evacuation was lifted, and my reputation for supplying the daily chuckle remained intact.

THE SHOOT DAY
Office/Set Communications

Filming has begun. Most of the daily action happens on set now. There is a different routine. You have to adapt to a new daily schedule. The set runs on time that does not really exist on a clock. Times like morning and afternoon are all relative to the start of your set day and set lunchtime. For example, 11:00 a.m. falls in your morning if the set started at 8:00 a.m., but it falls in the afternoon, if set started at 2:00 a.m.. Keep this in mind as you walk through the following explanation of a set day.

A. EARLY MORNING

Early morning for the office usually starts about 30 minutes before crew unit call time, or 9:00 a.m., whichever is earliest.

PUT COFFEE ON

First person in the office makes the first pot of coffee; like any other crew member, you will probably want a cup to start your day. Most people come to set or office before having had breakfast at home, and need a coffee to jump–start their day. Put a sign on or near the machine asking people to clean up after themselves, but expect to do the job anyway. Ceramic mugs are preferred to save trees and garbage dumps, but have some Styrofoam cups on hand for times when all the ceramic mugs are dirty, and guests come to visit.

HIRE DAILY STAFF

Have a list of Production Assistants and Secretaries handy so that you can call one in when one of your office staff calls in sick first thing in the morning. The A.D.s may also call from set to ask you to hire daily crew for other departments. For union positions, start with the union office. For nonunion positions, get preferred names from the department heads. It is for this purpose that you should meet and interview Production Assistants and

Secretaries even when you have no job to offer. You will have no time to interview crew that you call in on a daily basis. Note all of these daily crew names down on your copy of the call sheet or "to do" list so that you can send each one the correct deal memo paperwork, and you can be accurate in completing today's production report later.

CALL FOR A NEG REPORT

As mentioned before, call the lab (or have Post–Production call the lab) to get a report on the negative as soon as possible after processing. Forward the information, good or bad, onto the Production Manager.

FORWARD EXTRAS LIST TO SET

Extras Casting Directors often fax a list of Extras who will be reporting to set in the morning and at what times. Send this list to set with the first run, but keep a copy for yourself in case the original gets lost or delayed.

FIRST RUN (FROM SET)

Usually done by a Driver, the A.D.s should send you the draft copy of the production report with all its backup paperwork. If you do not have it by now, call set to ask for it. Review the entire package while the Driver is waiting, in case there are items that must be copied and returned to set immediately.

FIRST RUN (TO SET)

You likely already have items to return to set in the "to set" box. Some of those items are the draft call sheet (explained later in this chapter), and the extras list. Have the Driver wait for you to address the immediate requests that just came in the envelope from set. Ask Accounting if there is anything from their department that needs to be sent to set. Send all office/set packages to the A.D.s for distribution on set.

DAILY PRODUCTION REPORT

You get a draft from the A.D.s first thing in the morning. Check it over for accuracy and completion. Add to it any notes you made on your copy of the call sheet or "to do" list. Accounting will be grateful if you make sure daily crew names are listed. Photocopy the "corrected" draft copy for the A.D.s and Accounting. They need the form immediately. If you are new to production reports, review it with the Production Manager at this point. Then type it up for approval signatures by the First A.D. and the Production Manager. Once approved, you can finally distribute it to all who need it.

WHAT IS A PRODUCTION REPORT?

The daily production report is, quite naturally, a daily report from every department to Accounting and Executives on what transpired that day. Be clear in reporting everything from how much film and sound stock was used, to how long the film's running time is estimated to be, to the hours of all crew members and cast members, to general and specific notes about what happened on set. Remember that these are the documents that are examined in great detail if production ever has a legal battle or insurance claim, so fill them out accordingly. (See sample in the Appendix.)

B. MORNING

Morning is an hour to a few hours after call time.

SET CALLS IN FIRST SHOT

One of the A.D.'s will call when set has rolled film on the first shot of the day. Note this information down on your copy of today's call sheet. You will need this information to keep Producers and Executives informed, and to complete the production report tomorrow. Ask the Accountant, Production Manager, and Producer if they need to talk to set before hanging up.

C. MORNING AND/OR AFTERNOON

These events can happen in the "set" morning and/or the "set" afternoon. The timing of some items are up to your discretion; some will be dictated for you.

116

MAIL DELIVERY

When the mail comes in, open it, stamp it with the date received, and distribute it to the rightful recipients. Leave confidential mail sealed. Some people prefer their mail to be opened for them, others do not. Check with Producers, Production Manager, Accountants, Director, and Stars before doing so. Some productions will open fan mail for some performers (like children) to edit out any pieces that might be upsetting. Find out.

RUSHES TIME and PLACE

Coordinate with the post production team when and where yesterday's rushes will be screened. Keep the A.D.s informed of the changes as they happen throughout the day. Are there any people in head office you have to keep informed?

A.D.s CALL THE OFFICE

Whenever an Assistant Director calls the office to speak to anyone, ask where set is on the call sheet and note it down. Find out who, of the producing team, is presently on set. Refer to the notes you have been gathering in the "set square" by your telephone to make the conversation useful and brief. Chances are the A.D.s are calling from a cellular phone. Always check if the Producer, Production Manager, or Accountant needs to talk to set before hanging up.

HEAD OFFICE CALLS

Someone from a head office, a parent production company, or a co-production company may call, even on a daily basis to keep in touch with the production. The Production Manager will likely be the person of contact, but if he/she is not there, have some information to give. You talk to the A.D.s constantly. You know when first shot happened. You know if set has broken for lunch yet or not.

PUBLICITY EVENTS and VISITORS TO SET

As you coordinate events with Publicity or visitors to set, keep the A.D.s informed. As for publicity events, the A.D's need to know about these early so that they can arrange for time during the shoot day for Actors and/or Director to be available for interviews.

OFFICE PETTY CASH

The Office P.A. may need to do a petty cash report daily to avoid a float getting too low. Review it for enough detail before the Production Manager does, so you can answer any questions the P.M. may have about it later. Know what is happening in your department.

UNUSUAL TELEPHONE REQUESTS

The Producer may call you with unusual requests, like finding a monkey that can retrieve things on command, or finding fluorescent-colored contact lenses. These are requests that do not seem to fit into any department on the crew, so they fall into your lap. Here is where you can show creativity in researching the oddest of things. Refer to your kit of references books and you can find pretty much anything. If not, ask fellow Production Coordinators. Have fun!

VISIT THE SET

The Production Manager will visit the set on a daily basis. If you can do the same, do so. There is no better way of keeping in touch with what is happening on set than being there yourself. Use your visits to keep in touch with the crew, to gather information firsthand to aid you in completing the production report, or to get the latest production report signed very quickly.

REVIEW OTHER CHAPTERS

Chapter 8 ("A Form for All") has a list of supplies to check on a weekly basis. Use these checklists when the day allows. Chapter 10 ("Work with the Entire Crew") has lots of information about how to deal with each department. Review this from time to time. And Chapter 12 ("Countdown Through Production") identifies events before they are about to happen. Review this, too.

D. LUNCHTIME

Lunchtime means the crew is being catered a buffet lunch. The office often has to purchase their own lunch. If set is nearby, ask nicely for take-out.

SET CALLS IN LUNCH BREAK

The A.D.s will call when the set has stopped for lunch. Even if neither of you has any more news to offer, talk to each other. You may remember something during the course of a conversation.

E. AFTERNOON

Depending on how quickly the draft call sheet comes to you will determine how busy your afternoon will be.

THE FIVE O'CLOCK REPORT

This report rarely happens exactly at 5:00 p.m., but occurs after lunch and before wrap. An A.D. calls the Production Manager to report on the present filming status, and what is expected to be completed by the end of the day. This is your opportunity to get an estimated wrap time, or an approval to copy and distribute the call sheet.

CALL SHEET

After lunch, the A.D.s send you a draft handwritten copy of the call sheet for typing and copying. Show it to the Production Manager for approval and get a go-ahead from the A.D.s before copying it and distributing it to the many people who need it every day.

WHAT IS A CALL SHEET?

The call sheet tells the cast and crew when and where to show up on set the next morning and what weather is forecasted. It also informs everyone of what scenes are to be shot, and of what special requirements or daily crew each department must have arranged to accomplish the day. Finally, an advanced schedule of what is planned for the following day ends the call sheet. (See a sample in the Appendix.)

LOCATION MAP

The Locations Department will create a map to attach to the call sheet. If they cannot do this, make a map from the production office to location, depicting instructions in both pictures and words. Also note the closest hospital on the map, complete with address and emergency telephone number. Though scale can be approximate instead of exact, be very clear about your instructions. Imagine trying to drive to location at 3:00 a.m. to a place that you have never been to before. Print clear and large.

SIDES and SIDE COVER

Sides are selected pages from the script. For shooting on set, you need to reduce-photocopy sides to pocket-size for portability. Make them at the same time as you make the call sheet. Pull the pages from the script that correspond to the scenes on the call sheet, and reduce-photocopy them by 50 percent. Shrink the first page of the call sheet to use as a cover sheet. It informs the cast and crew what the planned shooting order of scenes is. Because sides are small, they often get treated as dispensable and get lost with great frequency. Label each set to the people that you and the A.D.s deem will need them on set.

CAST and CREW CALL FOR TOMORROW'S CALL TIME

Clear up with the A.D.s as to who is going to call whom with call times on a daily basis. You may call the Caterer and Extras Casting Director, while they may call the Cast, Stunt Performers, and Specialty Daily Crew. Some crew will call the office for call times without identifying themselves. Find out who you are talking to before handing out the "unit call time." These people may have a special call different from the majority of the crew. Write down their names and numbers. You may have to call these people again should the call time change later in the afternoon. Keep the A.D.s informed of who you have given call time information. Never let yourself give out the wrong call time.

F. LATE AFTERNOON

Call sheet for tomorrow done, you are now waiting for wrap. If set gets into overtime, the wait could be very long.

DRAFT CALL SHEET (FOR THE FOLLOWING DAY)

After the call sheet is completed, type a draft copy (with no times on it) for the following day to send to the A.D.s on set for completion tomorrow. Create this from the information on the advanced schedule and on the shooting schedule. This is a great time saver for A.D.s who do not have the luxury of a stationary desk and predictable weather on location.

G. AT WRAP

When the A.D.s call the office with "we've wrapped," it is not always time for you to go home. You may be in the office until you complete additional work.

SET CALLS IN WRAP TIME

Note wrap time on your copy of the call sheet, for reference when completing the production report tomorrow. At this point, they will also tell you if call time tomorrow is pushed or pulled or remains the same. If it stays the same, ask the A.D.s how long they need you to wait around the office after wrap. Someone may need access.

WHEN CALL TIME CHANGES

If tomorrow's call time has changed from the call sheet, (i.e., to one hour later), use a big fat red marker to write boldly at the top of all call sheets in your possession: "ALL CALLS + 1HR," then redistribute and re-fax it to everyone necessary. Next, telephone all heads of departments that are not on set with the new information. If it is too late to make telephone calls, leave a list for the person opening the office to make the calls in the morning. Double-confirm with the A.D.s who is calling whom with the call time change. Discuss with the A.D.s who is not on set or left set early and therefore needs a telephone call.

WHEN THE CALL SHEET REVISES TO PINK

Sometimes the changes to the call sheet at wrap are so extensive that you need to make a "pink revised" call sheet. This is the reason having a second person in the office until wrap is useful. Get the changes from the A.D.'s and type up the new call sheet as quickly as possible. Select and reduce-copy the new sides. Indicate in bold at the top of both the sides and the call sheet that these are "pink revised," so there is no confusion about which call sheet to use (even when faxed, or photocopied onto the wrong colored paper). If there is no Driver standing by, and if time permits, you or the Assistant may be charged with driving the new call sheet out to set.

You made it to the end of the day. That is a celebration in itself. Pat yourself on the back. Go home. Prepare two alarm clocks beside your bed (one on battery power, in case of power outages), and rest before you come back to tackle tomorrow. It is a different routine than prep, and perhaps a little more predictable in its form, so you will get used to it very quickly. Just remember that the cameras are rolling. You must be prepared for the unexpected.

The Customs Police

This is the story of how I nearly got arrested for carrying the wrong customs documents.

Enlisted to hand–carry a number of post elements to Los Angeles, I sat down in my plane seat — still on the tarmac in Toronto — and heard my named paged. The flight attendant told me that the company I worked for had just called the gate to tell me that I had the wrong elements, and did I know what that meant. I said yes, thanked her for the message, and asked to deplane. She said that it was too late and closed the door right in front of me. Since wrestling with her at this point would have been useless, I sat back down and resigned myself to a lovely, fruitless day of traveling to and from Los Angeles.

Upon my arrival at the Los Angeles airport, my contact examined the elements I brought and declared that all was well. I had the correct elements, but I just had too many. He gave me four items to return to Canada. Fine, I agreed, and looked at the customs documents in my hand. Written in clear, bold, underlined, block capital letters was the phrase: "Not to be returned to Canada." My contact gone, I called head office for advice.

They consulted their experts and reported back to me this simple procedure: "When you arrive in Canada at customs, the officer will examine the documents and arrest you." Arrest me? "Then he will take you to a holding room where we will have someone there to bail you out and clear the whole thing up." Arrest me? Great.

Fifty minutes later, I boarded the exact same plane to go back. I sat down and rehearsed over and over again what I might say to the customs officer for the next four and a half hours.

At customs in the Toronto airport, I handed over the offending document and spewed out as fast as possible, and in way too many words, my case along with an explanation of the events of my entire day. The customs officer interrupted me, returned the paperwork, and said he didn't want to hear my story. I should just go away. Speechless, I did just that.

Then I remembered that there was someone waiting for me in a holding room. I had to go back and ask in my sweetest, most innocent manner: "Uh, if you were to have arrested me, where might you have taken me?"

He paused before answering. I smiled. He told me. So I thanked him and trotted off to the holding room, entering it from the visitor's side (not the prisoner's side).

Upon my entrance, the promised contact was there, and she belted out fast and loud, "It's not her fault!" accompanying her declaration with grand gestures. The officers on duty regarded her with curiosity. I jumped in to shut her up, and dragged her out of the room to explain. I did not want the officers to change their minds about arresting me.

COUNTDOWN THROUGH PRODUCTION

Checklists for Production

You think about work day by day now. You initiated a lot of happenings during pre-production and are wondering what you can initiate during production. As a continuation of Chapter 4 ("Countdown to Production"), this chapter will count you down through the shooting period.

A. FIRST WEEK OF PRINCIPAL PHOTOGRAPHY

No doubt when shooting begins, you will still be tidying up things to do from pre-production. Along with those issues, address the following:

FIRST WEEK OF PRINCIPAL PHOTOGRAPHY

- ☐ Credits
- ☐ Crew Gifts
- ☐ Wrap or Outtake Reel

CREDITS

Though you may initially think this is too early to think about credits, know that credits will have to go through many drafts and approvals from many companies before they are final. Start a first draft for the Producer's and Production Manager's eyes only. Consult your crew deal memos, cast contracts, and any other information you have gathered in the credits file folder on your desk. Double–check all spellings. Call those people if you are at all unsure about the spelling of their names. Do not promise them a credit (you do not have the authority), just check the spellings. Credits are very sensitive information. Treat them with the utmost confidence.

CREW GIFTS

Crew gifts can be T-shirts, jackets, hats, bags, or doormats imprinted with the production name. Delivery of ordered items can take four to six weeks, so address this issue with the Producer and Production Manager early. Some productions will pay for the gifts, and others will sell them to the crew. Some productions want them to be a surprise, others do not. Find out, and order the items immediately. If the crew is to pay for all or part of the order, get payment in advance.

WRAP OR OUTTAKE REEL

Discuss with the Production Manager, Post–Production, and Continuity if you are going to create a wrap reel or outtake reel for the end of production. With enough notice, Continuity can note appropriate takes as they happen during the shoot for the editing team.

B. DURING PRODUCTION

Much of this is mentioned in Chapter 11 ("The Shoot Day"), but there are other issues that come up during production from time to time.

DURING PRODUCTION

☐ Call Sheet and Draft Call Sheet

☐ Daily Production Report and Backup

☐ Daily Equipment

☐ Daily Crew

☐ Stunt Contracts, Nurses, Ambulance Attendants

CALL SHEET and DRAFT CALL SHEET

Type up the call sheet as soon as possible, collect approvals, add the location map to it, make script sides, and distribute it.

DAILY PRODUCTION REPORT and BACKUP

The draft production report comes from the A.D.s in the first run of the morning. Check and complete it using the backup paperwork provided, and the information you gathered yourself yesterday. Collect approvals as necessary, type the form, get signatures, and distribute it. Treat it with confidentiality.

DAILY EQUIPMENT

Prepare purchase orders for any special equipment requests, remembering to gain approval from the Production Manager as you go.

DAILY CREW

Be prepared to call unions or suggested people first thing in the morning to replace absent crew members.

STUNT CONTRACTS, NURSES, AMBULANCE ATTENDANTS

If a Stunt Performer is scheduled for the next day, check that you have already completed his/her contract. Have you booked, or do you need, a Nurse or Ambulance Attendant?

C. TOWARD THE END OF PRINCIPAL PHOTOGRAPHY

Since you always must be ahead of the game, you must prepare for post-production and wrap before they happen, too.

TOWARD THE END OF PRINCIPAL PHOTOGRAPHY

- ☐ A.D.R. Sessions (Looping)
- ☐ Credits Continue
- ☐ Crew Gifts In
- ☐ Wrap List
- ☐ Wrap Party Prep

A.D.R. SESSIONS (LOOPING)

After an actor has completed filming, expect the post–production team to ask you to arrange an A.D.R. session ("Additional Dialogue Recording" or looping) for that actor. Post–Production may coordinate the studio, and you, the actor. Be sure that the proper time sheet or contract is completed at the session so the actor will be paid. Distribute a memo announcing the session and attendees.

CREDITS CONTINUE

Drafts and drafts of credits will continue to fill your files. If you do not get approvals from the people you need, call them to speed up the process.

CREW GIFTS IN

With luck, the crew gifts will be ready early. The easiest way to distribute them, whatever they are, is to label each gift with each crew member's name, and order them into alphabetical (but decorative) boxes. Imagine handing out 100 black sweatshirts to a crew that is working all over set. Unlabeled, the sweatshirts are identical and unidentifiable when crew members put them down temporarily as they work. Some will get lost. Few crew, if any, will mark their gift with their name as soon as they receive it. Also note that the Producer usually says a few words to the crew as gifts are being handed out.

WRAP LIST

Make a list of everything you have rented, leased, and bought during the course of production. You will have to return and sell all of it come wrap. The earlier you do the list, the more accurate it will be. Review it with the Production Manager.

WRAP PARTY PREP

Get a budget from the Production Manager for the event, and budget a party accordingly. Start to think about appropriate venues. (For more on wrap parties, see Chapter 21, "It's a Wrap.")

You can see the big picture of production and plan ahead. You find it not as daunting as you once did. But before you go too far into wrap, there are other ongoing issues that you need to explore further.

ON-GOING ISSUES

One Miracle, Please

Set called in a panic. They needed to change call time for a particular actor to two hours earlier. Today. The actor lived out of town and was no longer at home. He was somewhere in the city. I had to find him wherever he was and get him to set immediately. What am I, I thought, a miracle worker?

Think, think. Where could he be? I didn't know any of his friends. I didn't know what he likes to do on his time off. How does one go about finding someone who is just visiting a big city? Where was my crystal ball?

I mentally went over any casual conversation I'd had with him, and any conversation I'd overheard him have with someone else. Topics included acting, script revisions, the schedule, the weather. I needed something more personal. Sitting next to him at lunch one day, he had talked about getting into acting; about his home town; about a bar where he used to work in his home town. The bar was part of a chain. It was a long shot.

I got out the white pages and found that there were eight of these bars in town. Bar number one thought I was absolutely crazy to try to find him this way. I continued anyway. Bar number two thought I was crazy also, but the staff, surprised, actually found him there and brought him to the telephone.

When the actor got on the line, he obviously thought the bar was playing a joke on him. When I confirmed his identity and mine, and why I was calling, he was stunned to the point of near speechlessness. He would go to set immediately.

I hung up the phone, and paged the set to report the news. Then I sat back, a little stunned myself.

EVERYONE'S A STAR

Cast Contracts and Immigration

One of the file folders on your desk is labeled "cast contracts." It was a handy file to keep you abreast of the casting status as it happened, so you expect once the cast is contracted, the folder can be filed away. But the contracting process is taking longer than you expect. Then, one of the chosen actors needs an immigration permit...

A. AUDITIONS

The Casting Director and his/her company usually set up the auditions. Sometimes the job, or part of it, falls to you.

SET UP THE AUDITION SESSION

Arrange for a room or casting facility, a video camera, monitor, videotape, and a person to operate the video camera. The Casting Director will supply you with a list of attendees, what part they are reading for, and times they are coming. Copy this schedule for the Director, Producer, the Casting Director, the Video Operator, the Receptionist, and whoever else is going to be involved with the session. Keep a spare for your files.

MAKE AUDITION SIDES

Audition sides, like script sides, are selections of the script for reading during the audition. The Casting Director will choose which scenes for which character. Make copies, marking the character name boldly on the front page for all the appropriate Actors, for all the crew attending the session, and a few spares for on the day. Do not reduce-photocopy audition sides, and be careful in selecting the pages. For example, if a scene starts on a page before the character's lines start, you will likely need to copy the preceding page or two to give the Actor as much information about his/her character for the audition. Actors rarely get to read the entire script before auditioning. Give them as much help as possible.

DISTRIBUTE AUDITION SIDES

Once the sides are made, inform the Casting Director. He/she will arrange for Actors to come to the office to collect them. Some Agents will ask you to fax the sides to their office. Make absolutely sure that you give each Actor the right sides.

B. CAST CONTRACTS

You have a copy of the performers' union agreement. Read it. It may be dry reading, but it is essential that you are familiar with it. Attend any union/A.D. meeting in pre-production to meet the union representative.

1. Make A Draft Cast Contract
The Casting Director will send you a copy of each actor's deal memo. In pencil, draft a copy of the cast contract for each one on a photocopied union contract. Show both the deal memo and the contract to the Production Manager for approval. Then type it and gather signatures. Be aware that cast contracts incorrectly completed can cost the production unnecessarily large sums of money. Write them up carefully. Double–check your work.

STAR CONTRACTS

Star contracts are primarily done by Lawyers, but sometimes done by you with the Lawyer just checking them over. Stars are considered principal Actors by the union, but their rates are naturally above scale rates. Carefully read the deal memo provided by the Casting Director, then be very clear and very simple completing the draft "pencil" version of the contract. Let the Lawyers use legalese. Note on the union form all the information that relates to the A.D.s (like private dressing room provided), Transport (like transport to/from set) and Post–Production (one looping session included). Do not note any fees on this form but make an addendum. Addendums assure privacy of information. You can then copy the union form to the A.D.s showing the promises but not the money.

NONUNION CAST CONTRACTS

Most of the advice for completing union cast contracts still applies to nonunion cast contracts, but the form will be of your own making. If the Legal Department does not make the agreement for you, know that there are two separate items that you must buy from the performer: the performer's time on the work day, and the right to use the performer's recorded images and sounds afterward in the distribution of the production. Have a Lawyer review your form before use.

EXTRAS VOUCHERS

General Extras (or "Background Performers"), Special Skills Extras, and Stand-ins are cast by an Extras Casting Director and use Extra vouchers on set from the A.D.'s as their contracts. Sometimes you will be involved in finding Extras with specific special skills. Ensure the A.D.'s have enough vouchers for use on set.

2. Spelling
Some Assistants in casting offices do not spell Actors' names correctly. Double–check the exact spelling of the Actor's name with each Actor's Agent. Make sure the contract spells the name correctly because you will be referring to the contract when drafting up the credits. Nothing is more embarrassing than misspelling an Actor's name for the world to see.

3. List of Talent Agents
The union will have a list of Talent Agents. Obtain a copy. Cast contracts are always care of an agency address and telephone number. If the cast deal memos do not have complete talent agency information, the list you acquired will help you.

4. Agent vs. Manager
Some Performers have Talent Agents and Personal Managers. Talk to both. Find out where their jurisdictions lie. One may be in charge of contracts only, the other publicity. When you have a question, find out to whom you should speak first.

5. Type Rates Twice

Typing numbers are difficult. You do not have the luxury of spell check. Always type the performer's rate twice on a contract: once in numbers, and once describing the calculation. A daily rate written as $800.00 (scale plus 50%) and an hourly rate as $75.00 (scale) makes your intentions doubly clear, just in case you make a mistake in typing the numbers.

6. Work Permits

All nonunion performers working on a union production need work permits from the union. Starting Actors will pay for the permits themselves, and established Stars will likely have negotiated for production to pay for them.

7. Cast Contract Signatures

Check with the Production Manager, because sometimes it is the P.M. and sometimes it is the Producer who signs on behalf of the production company.

8. Distribute Cast Contracts

If the union form is 3-part carbon, each copy will note where to send them: the performer, the production company accounting office, and the union office. Make sure that the Legal Department and you also get copies. Assistant Directors often ask for copies as well in order to keep up with contracted promises. Mask the rates section for confidentiality.

9. Pictures and Resumes

Ask each Agent for pictures and resumes for each Cast Member on production. Publicity, Wardrobe, Hair and Makeup will be appreciative. Post your copies of the photographs in the production office with character names added to the bottom. For Stars, you may need extra copies for autographs. Discuss the performer's attitude toward autographs with the Agent.

10. Change of Dates Memos

If the dates as listed on the contract change, note the time and date you spoke with, and received confirmation from, the Agent or performer. Draft a memo detailing this confirmation and refer to the contract number (if applicable). Then copy the memo to all the people who receive the cast contract. The union agreement specifies how many hours notice is required for various changes and cancellations without penalty. Consider this memo to be a new addendum to the contract. By noting the time and date you spoke to the person, the memo becomes very useful to Accounting in determining if an Actor has to be paid for a day canceled or changed.

C. IMMIGRATION

Immigration permits can apply to both cast and crew. The following are procedures for bringing star performers across borders. If you are bringing in a crew member, adapt the information below.

1. Inform the Immigration Office
Warn the immigration office as soon as you know that a nonnational worker will be coming to work on the production. Give them the opportunity to be prepared for production to decide on a performer very shortly before filming begins. Discuss the latest procedures.

2. Collect Immigration Information
Collect this information from the Agent, the performer, or from yourself:

COMPLETE LEGAL NAME (some performers have stage names)

PERMANENT HOME ADDRESS

HOME TELEPHONE NUMBER (immigration may/may not need this)

AGENT'S ADDRESS (for the union work permit)

AGENT'S TELEPHONE NUMBER (for the union work permit)

DATE OF BIRTH

COUNTRY OF BIRTH

CITIZENSHIP

UNION WORK PERMIT(to prove union's permission)

JOB DESCRIPTION (character name and film title)

ARRIVAL TRAVEL DATE

FLIGHT COMPANY, FLIGHT NUMBER, ARRIVAL TIME, AIR TERMINAL and DEPARTURE TRAVEL DATE *

* Add at least two months to the departure date in case of an emergency. Otherwise, be prepared if production shoots an extra day or two after the permit has expired. You will have to take the performer across the nearest border to apply for another permit.

3. Pay for the Permit
In some countries, you have to get the performer to pick up and pay for the permit at the local embassy or consulate. In other countries you can meet the performer at the airport and pay for the permit on arrival.

4. Meet Performer at Airport
Whether the performer has the permit in hand or not, always have a representative of the production company to meet him/her at the airport. Be there for emergencies, hospitality, and for professionalism.

D. MORE ABOUT TRAVELING STARS

While you are asking questions of the Star for immigration purposes, find out his/her various preferences. You are probably the first person the performer will be dealing with on the production, so now is the time to make a good first impression.

HOTEL ROOM PREFERENCES

Ask about the hotel room preferences. Does the performer like a lot of, or little, sun exposure? Need a pool, fitness facility, smoking/nonsmoking room? Would he/she like to be in a particular area of town? Know your options before calling and promising the world.

AIRPLANE PREFERENCES

Does the performer want a smoking/nonsmoking seat, bulk head, aisle or window seat? Is there a frequent flyer number to attach to the ticket sale?

FOOD PREFERENCES and ALLERGIES

For Craft Service and Catering, ask about food preferences and allergies. Does the performer want a lot of fresh fruit, or does he/she have a penchant for dark chocolate? Are there any food allergies?

AUTOGRAPH PREFERENCES

If you have not already discussed how the performer likes to deal with autographs, discuss this now. You may be asked to store up the names of people who wish autographs so that the performer can sign them all at once at the end of the shoot.

SEND SCRIPT PACKAGE

As with any cast member, as soon as a Star is on board, send a script package with all the latest in paperwork from scripts to crew list to cast list. Include a personal letter of welcome, and if he/she has not traveled to your city before, include some travel information.

F. A.D.R. SESSIONS AND CONTRACTS

A.D.R. stands for "Additional Dialogue Recording," and is the recording of voices to match picture during Post-Production. A.D.R. is also known as "looping." Since A.D.R. usually happens after wrap, you may not have to deal with it, but if you are working on a series, you will.

1. Book and Contract Performers

Someone in Post–Production will likely be working with you to coordinate A.D.R. sessions. That person may arrange the studio, and you, the Actors. Make sure there is a signed contract for each Actor who is going to be recorded. Actors that have performed on set already have contracts. New voices may be added. Make these contracts as you would cast contracts. Refer to your union agreement, if applicable.

2. Performer Work Reports

As the A.D.s fill out work reports daily for the Actors on set to report what hours the talent worked, someone at the A.D.R. session must fill out the form for each session. Send a blank report to the session. You can help by filling in the production company name, title, date, and performers booked.

3. Make a Memo Announcing the A.D.R. Session

Send a memo confirming the details of the A.D.R. session to Post–Production, and to Accounting, Producer, and Production Manager. Accounting, now aware of the session, can track down the work report if it does not come back from the recording session promptly.

4. Keep A Copy of All Information

Keep a copy of all the information about the A.D.R. session in your desk file folder, in case you have to track down anything like missing work reports. Send a copy of all appropriate information to the performers' union office.

Cast Contracts seem overpowering when you first start working with them. They are legally binding and do promise a lot from production. Production Managers and Producers rely heavily on you to be accurate in their completion. Be sure you are.

PAID HOLIDAYS

Film shoots often work weekends and holidays to take advantage of location access and traffic patterns. Otherwise, they go on hiatus to avoid holidays. I can't remember the last time I was actually paid for a Christmas holiday. But there is one holiday-type day I do remember.

The director of the film was thrilled to find out I was a sailor with my own boat. One of the scenes was in front of the water, and he wanted a boat anchored in the background of the shot. He asked me to do the honors.

Sporting a bikini, I went to work with cel phone and walkie-talkie on board, and another sailor to give me a hand. We anchored the boat as instructed on the walkie-talkie to create optimal angle of the boat to the camera and then settled in for a day's relaxation. I didn't know what my orange bikini would look like from shore until the Director's voice came over the walkie: "Deb, are you wearing anything out there?" I must have looked naked. Oh boy. I quickly came back over the walkie: "Gee, was I supposed to?" And they all laughed. It was obviously not an issue, since the boat would be so far in the background.

So, for the day, I lounged aboard my sailboat, the sun shining, a sailor to bring me drinks, and getting paid! Then I wondered, how does one declare this on a time sheet?

COINS AND BILLS

Accounting Issues

You will delve into the land of accounting many times. Purchase orders and crew deal memos may mystify you at first, but now that you have succeeded in cast contracts, you will have no problem.

A. PURCHASE ORDERS (P.O.'s)

Few people admit they know nothing about how the purchase order system works, yet it is critical to everyday accounting.

WHAT IS A PURCHASE ORDER?

A purchase order (when signed by the Production Manager) is a promise that the production will pay the price listed for the goods or service ordered, even though no invoice has been created yet. Purchase order in hand, Accounting can set aside the money promised and not spend it elsewhere. Treat purchase orders like contracts. Be detailed so that the Accountant will be able to match the purchase order to the invoice when the invoice arrives days, weeks, or months later.

PRICE CHANGES

The objective of the purchase order is to prevent the supplier from invoicing a higher price than originally agreed, but sometimes there are extenuating circumstances and a price changes. Find out about these situations before invoicing happens. Then distribute a "canceled" version of the first purchase order, and create a new one with the correct price.

WHO GETS COPIES OF PURCHASE ORDERS

Once signed by the Production Manager, just like a contract, a copy of the P.O. should go to the supplier, to Accounting, and to you.

BE DETAILED

Put as much information as possible on the P.O. to prevent misunderstanding. Describe the item, the purchase or rental conditions, and rental period. Mention if tax is or is not included. Note which department is initiating the purchase, and for which episode and/or set it is going to be used. If there is a work order number to refer to, use it. Any and all of this information will help the Accountant to match the purchase order to the invoice when it arrives. Do not forget to note today's date.

LOG THE P.O.'s

Log as much of that information as you can on your P.O. log form (as previously described). When you want to refer to a particular purchase or rental later, you will find that your P.O. log is much more efficient than sifting through stacks and stacks of P.O.s.

SIGN OUT P.O.s

Have crew members sign out prenumbered purchase order forms from you. Note on your log form who has each series. Now you can track down any blank P.O.'s with as much vigor as signed ones.

EXPLAIN HOW THE PURCHASE ORDER SYSTEM WORKS

Take the time to explain to the crew how P.O.s work. You may have to do this a few times, but you will find the effort worth it, and Accounting will be grateful.

B. CREW DEAL MEMOS

Another of the active file folders on your desk is the "crew deal memos" folder. The faster you get people to sign deal memos, the faster you can create a crew list and know that production is underway.

P.M. MAKES THE DEAL

The Production Manager will talk to the crew one by one and strike a deal with them. Ask daily who is on board and needs a deal memo. Not everyone will know where to get deal memo forms.

HAVE CREW SIGN DEAL MEMOS

Some crew will miss signing their own deal memos. Some will miss filling out a deal memo altogether, but still expect to be paid on schedule. Use a crew list as a top sheet to track whose deal memo you have and whose has yet to be completed. Note that some crew will take their deal memo straight to Accounting, or leave it in the Production Manager's office. It is your job to see they all get done. Keep copies for your files, signed and unsigned, in case any get lost in the flow from your desk to the Production Manager's for signature to Accounting's for use and filing.

DEAL MEMOS ARE CONFIDENTIAL

Some crew will not want you to see their deal memos, even though you are in charge of coordinating them all, and distributing them to the appropriate departments and unions. Be patient and get a copy of their deal memos from Accounting later, if need be.

DOUBLE–CHECK DEAL MEMOS ARE COMPLETE

Before you get the Production Manager to sign a large stack, check over the deal memos for completeness. Be sure the crew member has signed, rates are noted, and proper permit papers attached, if applicable. Some crew may even fill in the wrong union's deal memo form and not notice. Determine a crew rate sheet from the Production Manager, and keep one at your desk for easy reference.

HAVE DEAL MEMOS SIGNED IN BUNCHES

Gather a collection of deal memos together for the Production Manager to sign at your daily meetings. This will save the P.M. the time of having each crew member ask for a signature individually.

WHEN THE CREW MEMBER IS A CORPORATION

Since crew members travel from production to production, contract to contract throughout the year, they are generally freelance, and can incorporate as a business. A corporation means the crew member has a company name that ends with Inc., Incorporation, Corp., Corporation, Ltd., Limited, or Unlimited. Accounting will need a copy of their corporate top sheet as proof, and likely will have another form or two to complete. Hand these forms out with the deal memo.

WHEN THE CREW MEMBER IS AN EMPLOYEE

Employee status means that Accounting will be making source deductions from the crew member's paycheck. The production company is the crew member's employer. Obtain plenty of tax forms from the nearest tax office. Filled out, these tell Accounting which tax category to use for each employee.

WHEN THE CREW MEMBER IS NOT A CORPORATION

In most cases, if crew members are not incorporated, they must be treated like employees. They cannot invoice like companies. Ask Accounting to explain the tax reasons to crew members who insist on being "employees that invoice."

WHO RECEIVES COPIES OF DEAL MEMOS

Treat deal memos like any other contract. Send copies to Accounting, your files, the appropriate union, and to the crew member. Ask the Legal Department if they need a copy of any of them. When sending the copy to the crew member, place it in an addressed, sealed envelope. Like all contracts, they are confidential.

HOW TO FILE DEAL MEMOS

As production continues, you will be handling numerous deal memos. Even daily crew need one each. Highlight the crew member's last name (not the corporation name) and file them alphabetically. If anyone ends up with a deal memo in two different departments, you will find both deal memos together in an alphabetical setup. Note on your crew list cover sheet which deal memos are completed.

MORE ABOUT DAILY CREW

Keep a log of all daily crew, their job, and their phone number. You can attach a sheet to the back of your crew list with this information. Copy it for the A.D.s and for Accounting, too. Daily crew work so briefly that they can easily be forgotten in the flow of paper and not get paid. The list will also jog the A.D.'s and your memory of good daily crew for future reference.

WRAP DEAL MEMOS AT THE VERY END

At some time during production you will have all the deal memos of all the main crew, and you will feel comfortable enough to file this desk folder into the cabinet. Do not remove it from your desk so hastily. Production will be hiring dailies right up to, and during, wrap. Even you will probably be hiring a daily P.A. to help set up the wrap party.

C. SUPPLIER LETTERS OF AGREEMENT

When the Production Manager informs you of a verbal deal he/she made with a supplier (like the Caterer or Casting Director), you should create a letter of agreement immediately to confirm the details.

HOW TO PREPARE A LETTER OF AGREEMENT

Be simple and direct. Use letterhead to type a letter to the supplier, including their name, address, telephone, and fax numbers. Address the letter to the person who will be signing his/her agreement to the deal. Start the letter with: "This letter confirms the following:" and then proceed to explain very plainly the details of the agreement; what the production company is promising; and what the supplier is promising. End with: "Your signature below indicates your agreement to the above," and mark spaces for the Production Manager and the supplier's representative to sign. Make copies for yourself, Accounting, the supplier, and the Legal Department on all these letters.

WHEN TO USE LETTERS OF AGREEMENT

Letters of agreement can be for Caterers, Casting Directors, someone giving permission to use his/her name in the script, or even nonunion crew members. The options are endless.

CONFIRM FORM WITH P.M. OR LEGAL

Let the Production Manager review all letters of agreement before sending them out for signature. Depending on the complexity of the letter, the P.M. may elect to forward it on to the Legal Department for rewording. Your simple phrases will be a terrific start for a more formal contract. Collect the wordings of successful simple letters of agreement for reference on future productions.

WHERE TO FILE LETTERS OF AGREEMENT

If these letters are with crew members, file with the crew deal memos. If they concern clearances or the contact list, file them with the clearances or the contact lists respectively.

Nearly everything in production has a price attached to it, therefore nearly everything in production relates to Accounting. Principal photography is the point in a film's life when most of the money gets spent in a very condensed period of time. The more you can help the Accountant, the better. Become a friend of Accounting.

I Won't Go Back to White

When it comes to revising a script, I hate going back to white. I will search high and low for every pastel-colored paper on the market to postpone the inevitable "return to white."

It was very close to end of production, and I was happy that we had never had to return to white. We had survived numerous script changes, and I was certain the revisions were at an end. We had been from white to pink to blue to green to yellow — the standards. Then on to buff to salmon to gray to goldenrod to sand and at last to lavender.

Then one more revision came in. It was a short two-pager. I couldn't bear the thought of going back to white for such a short revision, but we had exhausted every pastel paper on the market. So, I got out red and green highlighters, and with the help of the office staff drew a pattern on each page to publish... the plaid revisions.

THE SCRIPT IS A RAINBOW

Script Format and Revisions

Keeping up with script revisions seems like trying to catch a waterfall. Impossible! As soon as you return from the photocopier with one colored revision, another awaits you atop your desk. You know, however, there must be a way to keep up with the ever-changing script.

A. FORMATTING THE EARLY DRAFTS

There are many wonderful books on the market that can explain script formatting in great detail. This chapter will not attempt to replace them, but will present you with a nutshell version of what you need to know or learn. As the Production Coordinator, you must know script format better than even the Writing Department. A well-formatted script is essential to explain the story clearly and easily to the crew for filming.

1. Choose A Script Format
Of the several formats used, and endless versions on those formats by Writers and Producers, choose between two of the basic kinds: feature film format and comedy format. Get the Writing Department's and Producer's approval in choosing a script format.

2. Who Types The Script
The fastest typist in the office should type scripts on the condition that he/she is also the person who best understands script format. Reformatting pretyped pages takes almost as long as retyping an entire script.

3. Make Format Consistent
Be consistent about labeling scene locations, about identifying character names, about everything. This advice cannot be repeated too many times. The reason: if a script notes Laura's living room as "Laura's Living Room," "Living Room," "Interior Laura's House," and as "The Fisher Living Room," the crew will be confused over how many locations the script actually needs.

4. Inform Crew of Changes While Typing

When you type the script, you are reading it word for word. You are bound to notice, for example, that seven new props have been added to a certain scene. Note this down and talk to the Props Department soon to find out if they are aware of the change. Since the script itself will take a few more hours to type, print, copy and distribute, informing the crew as you type can give them added time to address the new changes.

WHAT TO LOOK FOR   WHO TO TELL

Changes that affect today	Appropriate Department(s)
Changes that affect tomorrow	Appropriate Department(s)
New characters	Producer/Casting Department
Changed character names	Clearance Company/Legal Department
Changed location names	Clearance Company/Legal Department
New locations	Locations Department
New props	Props Department
New wardrobe	Wardrobe Department
New action (stunts, effects)	Appropriate Department(s)
Changed dialogue	Actors affected

5. If You Are Not The Typist

If you choose a typist other than yourself, have a copy of the source file (or handwritten script pages) to read as the typing is happening. Keep on top the revisions. Make notes. Inform the crew.

6. Typing From Various Formats

Writers will give you scripts on anything from computer disk to handwritten sheets of paper torn from a binder. Especially on a series, it is your job to make each script format the same.

TYPING FROM HANDWRITING

If the writers give you a script in handwritten form, you will learn to be very good at reading their individual handwriting. Most writers are so eager to get the idea onto paper, that proper spelling and grammar are sometimes overlooked. In this case, do not always type word for word. Read the script as you type to determine if the "mistake" you are reading is an intentional style of writing or a typo. Proper scene breaks can be missing, too. Do not have characters walk from room to room or flash forward in time without breaking for a new scene heading.

TYPING FROM DISK

Even if the script is given to you on computer disk, the writer's word processing program may not be the same as yours. When translating the file into your word processor, you will either find yourself reformatting the entire script or, at worst, needing to retype every word. Whichever you do, print out a copy for the Producer first, then read the script as you work to be sure correct scene breaks occur.

TYPING FROM MODEM-SENT FILE

If you and the Writer do not have compatible word processing programs, the file you receive over the modem will likely be in ASCII or DOS text. All word processing format will be lost in the modem transfer. Print out a copy for the Producer to review as is, then begin the process of turning the text into a script.

7. When Not To Reformat or Retype

The Producer may suggest that you do not reformat or retype the first script that you receive from the Writer. He/she may want to radically revise the script in its present state. Save yourself the work, and find out.

8. If You Need Help Formatting

If you are worried about script format, or you have a question about where to break a scene or how to number a scene, go to the Assistant Directors. They have to schedule the script scene by scene, and can advise you.

9. When Is A Draft Final?

All early (prefinal) drafts should not have scene numbers. Only when the script is called a "Final Draft" by the Producer should you number the scenes. This system ensures that the crew does not do massive breakdowns of what they need for their respective departments on a draft of the script that has yet to go through more major changes. Keep in touch with the Producer and the Writers about how close to "final" the script is.

10. Who Numbers The Scenes?

Some A.D.s like to number the scenes in the script. Most expect the Coordinator to do the job. If you are unsure about how to number a sequence, ask the A.D.s. You have the knowledge of script formatting, and they have the knowledge of how they plan to shoot this collection of scenes.

11. Save At Least Two Copies

The script in your computer is a long document. Save it, and a backup copy. If you do not, just imagine having to type the whole script over again from scratch. Keep backups of each draft in case long sections of deleted script reappear in later revisions.

B. TITLE PAGES

There are about as many versions of title pages as there are version of script formats. Be clear. Be consistent.

TITLE and WRITING NAMES

Center the title and writing names, and place them about a third of the way down from the top of the page. The title is underlined or quoted. Identify all the writers of the project in correct credit spelling and contractual order. If in doubt, check with the Producer.

PRODUCTION COMPANY NAME, ADDRESS, and TELEPHONE

To identify ownership of the property, note the production company name, address, and telephone number at the bottom right or bottom left of the title page.

SCRIPT STATUS and DATE

Is the script a first, second, final draft, or pink revision? For early drafts, type which early draft and the date. For any script after final draft, include all the revisions and dates in a growing list. This list will remind crew of all the different parts they need to make a single complete script. Place the list at the top right or bottom right of the title page. Leave enough room for at least twelve different colored revisions.

COPYRIGHT AND/OR DISCLAIMER

Some production companies require a copyright notification and/or a disclaimer on the title page. Ask the Producer. If you need one, place it at the bottom center of the page. If it is long, type it in small print.

SAMPLE TITLE PAGES

Since pictures can speak more than words, the following two pages depict sample title pages from a heavily revised single production script, and an early draft of one episode of a series.

```
        FINAL (WHITE) DRAFT  -   1 December 2001
        PINK REVISED         -   2 December 2001
        BLUE REVISED         -   3 December 2001
        GREEN REVISED        -   4 December 2001
        YELLOW REVISED       -   5 December 2001
        ORANGE REVISED       -   6 December 2001
        BUFF REVISED         -   7 December 2001
        TAN REVISED          -   7 Dec 2001 (PM)
        GOLDENROD REVISED    -   8 December 2001
        LAVENDER REVISED     -   8 Dec 2001 (PM)
        WHITE AGAIN REVISED  -   9 December 2001
    *   PINK AGAIN REVISED   -  10 December 2001
```

"Script Revision Nightmare"

written by

Deborah S. Patz

based on a story by

Laura J. C. Fisher

Production Company Ltd.
Production Company Address
Production Company Telephone
Production Company Fax Number

Copyright notice & disclaimer

SCRIPT REVISION NIGHTMARE

Episode #2

"Oh No! Not Again!"

teleplay by

Deborah S. Patz

based on characters by

Laura J. C. Fisher

Second Draft - 26 April 2005

Production Company Ltd.
Production Company Address
Production Company Telephone
Production Company Fax Number

Copyright notice & disclaimer

C. FEATURE FILM SCRIPT FORMAT

This format can be used for feature films, movies of the week and any type of drama program. It can also be used in a series format, but in this case, assume that the production is solitary.

PAGER HEADER

For page one, center the title at the top of the page. Specify the color and date of the latest revision at the top right. For all other pages, make a header at the top left that reads title, color, and date. This redundancy is especially important to identify pages when they are faxed, copied onto the wrong-colored paper, or found separated from the script.

PAGE NUMBERS

Scene numbers and page numbers can be similar or even identical, depending on the pace of the script. If you use a dash before and after page numbers, you will find it harder to mistake page numbers for scene numbers (which are also on the right side of the page).

TAB SETTINGS

Listing them from left to right, these are the tab settings you will need:

-0.5" left of left margin	Scene #
-Left margin	Scene Headings & Action
-1" in from left margin	Dialogue
-2" in from left margin	Parenthetical
-2.5" in from left margin	Character Name
-5" in from left margin	Transitions
-0.5" in from right margin	Page #
-Flush Righ	tScene #, Revision Marks

SCENE HEADINGS

Make scene headings bold and in capitals so that you and the crew can find them quickly. Scene headings are made up of three parts: inside/outside; where; when. Begin with "Int." (Interior) or "Ext." (Exterior), then describe the location, use a dash, and end with "Day" or "Night." Always include all three parts. Read the script carefully, if need be, to gather the information for all three parts. Do not use more than one dash. If you use formatting software, dashes may be indications that the location description is completed and the information after the dash will be considered the time of day. And finally, be consistent about the location descriptions. Do not give one location more than one description.

SCENE NUMBERS

Place scene numbers far into the margins at both sides of the page for fast, double reference. Precede the number with "Sc." so that crew will quickly differentiate between them and the page numbers.

ACTION

Description of action is generally very sparse in a script. Ensure you use hard returns at the end of each line instead of letting the computer do the line scrolling. This will be useful when you come to revise the script line by line.

WHEN TO CAPITALIZE IN ACTION

Character names, technical action, and sounds can be capitalized, but with action description being sparse, capitalizing words can get out of hand.

-Character Names

Capitalize a character name only the first time the character appears in a scene. This will help crew to determine who plays in the scene.

-Technical Action (left margin)

Terms like Angle On, Different Angle, Music, SFX (Sound Effects), SPFX (Special Effects) are all capitalized and placed on the left margin for notice. These are specific requirements of camera, sound, and other technical departments.

-Technical Action (within description)

When technical effects are not highlighted by placing them on the left margin and are written in the middle of a descriptive paragraph, capitalize the feature for notice. These include: BANG!, LIGHTS ON, etc.

DIALOGUE

Dialogue margins are rather flexible. How wide or narrow they are depends on the intended pace of the dialogue. Discuss this with the Producer or Writing Department. As with the action, use hard returns at the end of each line so that later you can revise each line individually.

CHARACTER NAMES

Capitalize all character names and be consistent. The script may give a character several names throughout the course of the story, but you should let each character have only one name. If a character changes names during the script, keep using one name and later in the script, add the new name in brackets beside the character name. Do not center character names if you are using any formatting software, because the software relies on specific tab settings to find the character names.

PARENTHETICAL

You will see words in brackets beside character names and under character names. Parentheticals are the ones underneath and they are descriptions of how the dialogue is to be read, or what is to be acted simultaneously.

TERRY
-How words are said   [Whispers]
-To whom words are said   [To computer]

-Toward where words are said   [To offscreen]

-Actions to be performed   [Waves hand]

-Laughter and sighs   [Chuckles]

Directions in brackets beside the character name, are production explanations, not directions for the actor.

-The dialogue continues   TERRY [CONT]

-Location of the character   WOMAN [ON TV]

- Speech is voice–over or narration   MAN [V.O.]

-Dialogue is heard from offscreen   VOICE [O/S]

-Alternate character name   COORDINATOR [TERRY]

TRANSITIONS

Transitions are editing commands that carry you to an entirely different scene. These include: Cut To, Dissolve, Swish Pan To. Do not confuse these with on–set technical commands, like "Angle On," that instruct you to a new camera angle in the same scene.

CONTINUED

Note "continued" in brackets at the bottom of one page and top of the next when a scene continues onto another page. This makes each page clear about whether the scene ends here. When noting "continued" at the top of the next page, add the scene number for clarity.

SCRIPT PAGE SAMPLE

The following two pages depict a sample of all the formatting notes mentioned above, plus revision asterisks.

"Script Revision Nightmare"   Blue - 3 Dec 2005

FADE IN

Sc.1 **EXT. OFFICE BUILDING - NIGHT**   Sc.1

The office building is rather run-down. A pale light emanates from
one window in the darkened building.

                        COORDINATOR (V.O.)
                I can't take it any more!

                                              CUT TO:

Sc.2 **INT. COORDINATOR'S OFFICE - NIGHT**   Sc.2

The COORDINATOR sits at a desk. The only light in the room is from
the one on the desk and the glow of the computer screen. The
Coordinator looks harried and taps a few more keys. The computer
BEEPS in return.

                        COORDINATOR
                        (weakly)
                Come on, don't do this to me. I have to get
                this revision out in an hour! Please?   *

BIG FLASHING LIGHTS come from the computer. The Coordinator jumps
back and takes cover behind a filing cabinet.

                        COORDINATOR (CONT)
            Wha-?

The light show ends. The Coordinator looks out from behind the
filing cabinet. The Coordinator is not pleased.

ANGLE ON: COMPUTER SCREEN. It is blank.   *

                        COMPUTER VOICE
                Whew! That feels better!

ANGLE ON: COORDINATOR, perplexed.   *

                                              (CONTINUED)

158

"Script Revision Nightmare" - Pink Again - 10 Dec 94   -2-

2. CONTINUED:

                    COORDINATOR
        I must be mad. I could swear you just talked.

                    COMPUTER VOICE
        Who? You mean me? Sure did, Terry.

As the computer talks, SMALL FLASHES OF LIGHTS buzz across the
screen. The Coordinator comes out from behind the filing cabinet and
is mesmerized by the discovery.

                    COORDINATOR (TERRY)
        And how long have you lived in there?

                    COMPUTER VOICE
        Hard to say, since I define time a little
        differently from you guys.

                    COORDINATOR (TERRY)
        Can you... uh... format scripts?

                    COMPUTER VOICE
        Oh, please. You need to ask? I'm your computer,
        of course I can. What's the mystery?

The Coordinator sits down, intrigued.

                    COORDINATOR (TERRY)
        Then, maybe we should form a team. I give you   *
        a nice raw script, and you format it into a
        nice film format. What do you think?

                    COMPUTER VOICE
        Hmmm. You mean no more wandering aimlessly
        through the Internet? You'd even invite me
        into your world and everything?

                    COORDINATOR (TERRY)
        Well... I'd sure do what I can.

                    COMPUTER VOICE
        This could be a rather interesting deal...

The Coordinator picks up the latest script revision file. Inside it
there is a computer disk.

END TEASER

D. COMEDY SCRIPT FORMAT

This format can be used for comedy, sit-coms, or any fast-paced dialogue scripts. Since single episode productions have already been addressed, assume that the comedy script is for a television series. Basically, use the same format as the feature film script format, incorporating a few changes.

PAGE HEADER

Add the episode number to the header. With a series, you will be handling revisions for many episodes at the same time, and will need to identify each page separately.

ACTION

Action is completely capitalized for this type of format.

DIALOGUE

Dialogue is still uppercase and lowercase, but is double–spaced for easy, fast reading.

SAMPLE

The following page shows the differences between the feature film script format and the comedy script format.

4. CONTINUED:

> TERRY
> (sighs)

> I do believe, Compy, that you took that

> entirely the wrong way.

> COMPY
> I don't think so.

> TERRY
> Well, I know you did.

> COMPY
> Did not.

> TERRY
> Did too.

> COMPY THE COMPUTER
> Well! If that's the way you feel, I think

> I'll just go and fly the Internet and find

> a nice place for a well-earned holiday until   *

> you realize the truth and apologize.

COMPY LEAVES IN A FLURRY OF LIGHTS AND BUZZES. TERRY IS ANNOYED.

> DISSOLVE TO:

Sc.5 **INT. COORDINATOR'S OFFICE - NIGHT (LATER)**   Sc.5

TERRY SITS ALONE IN FRONT OF THE COMPUTER. NO MATTER HOW MUCH
TAPPING TO THE KEYS, COMPY IS NO WHERE TO BE FOUND.

> TERRY
> Ah, geez, Compy. I didn't mean it. What

> can I say? Come back, will ya?

A FLASH OF LIGHT PASSES, BUT IT IS ONLY THE PASSING OF A POLICE CAR
OUTSIDE.

> CUT TO:

E. SCRIPT REVISIONS

When you revise a script, you need to highlight to the crew exactly what has changed without asking them to read the entire script every time. Here is a step-by-step process to keep on top the many revisions that flood your desk.

1. Collect Script Revisions In Desk File Folder
You collect notes for script revisions from many sources. The Producer and Writing Department give you marked-up copies of the script. You have taken notes during production meetings as future script changes are discussed. You have notes from the script clearance company about changes that need to be made. You have heard the A.D.s mention that a scene will be shot in a different way from what was originally written. Make a note about this, too. Store all your notes in the desk file folder labeled "script revisions." When you come to revise the script, all your notes will be in one place.

2. Who Approves The Revisions
Though revisions and requests for revisions come in from far and wide, they must all be approved by the Producer. Review them with him/her.

3. When To Revise A Script
Publish a new script or new set of pages only when there are enough revisions to warrant publishing, or when the change is drastic enough to require that you inform the crew immediately. Ask the Producer. If you have been informing the crew of changes before they happen, publishing the pages daily or hourly is not crucial.

4. Revised Pages vs. Revised Script
Consider the number of pages that you need to revise. If revised pages account for more than 70 percent of the script, you will do better to publish an entire new draft on the new color, reformatting the pages as you go. You cannot, however, revise an entire script once shooting has begun. Continuity is using the script as is to make notes to the editors.

5. Typing The Revisions
When it is time to revise the script, here is how to type it:

CHANGE THE TITLE PAGE

Add the new revised color and date to the list of revisions on the title page.

CHANGE THE PAGE HEADER

Change the header on each page to note the correct new color and date for the revision.

MAKE CHANGES AND MARK NEW REVISIONS

Every time you change a word in the script, mark the changed material with an asterisk (*) flush right on that line. There is no limit to the number of asterisks you can use on a page. With this system, crew can immediately find the new material on the revised page.

REVISING A REVISION — CLEAR OLD REVISION MARKS

Before revising a script that has been previously revised, erase all previous revision marks (asterisks). If not, you will find a buildup of asterisks, and finding the latest revision on the page becomes increasingly difficult.

SOFT RETURNS VS. HARD RETURNS

Because you revise the script one line at a time, you need hard returns at the end of each line to allow you to flush right and place the asterisks. If soft returns (the computer's automatic line-scrolling) are still in the script at this point, search and replace them with hard returns.

A & B SCENES

Once a script is marked "final," the scene numbers cannot change. To insert new scenes in between two existing ones (like scene 6 and 7), you must number the new scenes with A's and B's i.e., Sc.6, Sc.6A, Sc.6B, Sc.7. Hopefully, you will never have to insert a scene between scene 6A and 6B. If you do, try: Sc.6A, Sc.6AA, Sc.6B.

OMITTED SCENES

Once a scene is added to the script it must always be listed, even if it is omitted. Like any scene header, note the scene number and "omitted" beside. Keep this notification in every revised draft that follows.

A & B PAGES

As the scene numbers remain fixed in a "final" draft script, so do the page numbers. If the revised page becomes shorter due to omissions, leave the rest of the page blank. If the revised page becomes longer, continue the revision on an "A" page. Your page numbers can therefore look like this: page 12, 13, 14, 14A, 14B, 14C, 15, 16, etc.

OMITTED PAGES

When the new material causes you to remove one or several pages from the script, mark the span of page numbers missing atop one of the revised pages. Your new page number sequence could, therefore, look like this: page 12, 13-14B, 14C, 15, etc.

If you need to research more about typing scripts, do so. You will be looked at as the resident expert on the subject. With common sense, you may find that you know more about script formatting and revisions than you think. All you have to do is be clear, and highlight the important information. Then you will be away to the — uh, photocopy machine.

What Meaneth Nine to Five?

There is nothing whatsoever nine to five about working in film - except, maybe, one thing.

Renting an ice rink in the middle of hockey season means that you have to travel to work at 2:30 in the morning with the radio in your car cheerfully saying, "And here's a song to get you home safely tonight."

When the boiler breaks in the production office at 3:00 a.m., you won't be able to get in touch with the landlord before seven or eight o'clock. String all baseboard heaters into the smallest office you can, and gather any people in the office for that early morning huddle. Keep your parkas on for added warmth. Draw straws to find out who is the next person to walk down the icy hallway to make the next photocopy.

Then, think about it. Who is going to call the production office at 3:30 in the morning? The set. Go to the set with the Production Manager. It's an ice rink. It's bound to be warmer. Just remember to be back in time to arrange for the fixing of the boiler.

Have lunch at nine in the morning, and an afternoon snack around noon. Start fading about three o'clock, but the end of the work day is nearing. Be prepared for this. Driving home is one of the few times you get to mingle with all those nine-to-fivers. It's five o'clock rush hour.

WHEN IT ALL HAPPENS

Production Scheduling

You hear the word "schedule" and wonder if it is a pre-production schedule, production schedule, one-line schedule, or shooting schedule. The Assistant Directors seem to schedule everything, and you have to get that information to the crew. You want to be up to speed on each type of schedule.

A. PRE-PRODUCTION SCHEDULE

Pretty much every day in prep the Assistant Directors revise a list of the events that are scheduled to happen during pre-production. This list includes times of meetings, location surveys, and wardrobe fittings and is usually drafted in the form of a memo. It is your job to distribute the memo to the crew daily. If given to you handwritten, you are to type it up also.

B. PRODUCTION SCHEDULE

This schedule you make yourself. Collect information from the Production Manager, Producer and/or A.D.s to generate a week–by–week breakdown of the entire production's schedule and try to fit it on one page. Note each week if the production is in prep, shooting, on hiatus, on holiday, or wrapping. Also note which days of the week are shoot days. At a glance the crew can now understand the entire schedule, even which weeks are non-Monday-to-Friday workweeks. When this schedule revises, copy it onto colored paper just like a script revision for notice. Long after production has concluded, the Accounting, Publicity, and Legal Departments will be referring to this schedule. Be accurate. Here is a hypothetical example:

MON.SEP.01	Labor Day Holiday (off)
TUE.SEP.02 — FRI.SEP.05	Prep
SUN.SEP.07 — THU.SEP.11	SHOOT EPISODE #1
MON.SEP.15 — FRI.SEP.19	Hiatus
MON.SEP.22 — FRI.SEP.26	SHOOT EPISODE #2
MON.SEP.29 — FRI.OCT.03	Wrap

C. THE PRODUCTION BOARD (STRIP BOARD)

The A.D.s create the shooting schedule by first making a production (or strip) board. The board can be a physical board, or created on computer. If it is a physical board, it is large and black, and when opened, displays many colored vertical strips coded with numbers and words. There is also a large white "header board" that displays the legend for the number codes. The entire board is written in pencil. Become familiar with looking at and reading a board. Since the A.D.s are the ones that create the board, you do not need to know all the details of creating one yourself. But since the board always depicts the schedule in its latest form, you should know some of the basics.

EACH STRIP IS A SCENE IN THE SCRIPT

Each colored strip on the board represents one scene of the script, no matter how long each scene is. Though the information on each strip can vary from A.D. to A.D., you can read on each strip the scene number, whether the scene is day or night, a written description of the location, a microsynopsis of what happens in the scene, and a list of each character in that scene (with each character represented by a number code).

THE HEADER BOARD

The header board is the first panel of the board and it tells you the film title, key crew names, the version of the script used for this schedule, and a legend of which character has been assigned to which character number. These character numbers you use on the cast list and the call sheets.

WHY DIFFERENT COLORS FOR EACH STRIP

The colors of each strip tell you at a glance if the scene is day or night, interior or exterior. A legend that is often used is:

- White: Exterior day (think bright light, like the sun, appears white)

- Yellow: Interior day (think the color of household lights are yellowish)

- Blue: Exterior night (think films often light night scenes blue)

- Green: Interior night (think yellow "interior" plus blue "night" equals green)

Black and red strips serve as borders between the days. Red identifies a weekend. Black strips usually have a white space to summarize the date and total the number of pages scheduled to be shot for that day. Every strip is written in pencil, since the board changes with every script revision.

WHY DIVIDE THE PAGES BY EIGHTHS

You see the scene page counts listed in eighths of pages and wonder why would anyone choose fractions that are difficult to add and subtract to use as numerical totals. Eighths are actually a good fraction for division. You can divide a page in half, and in half again, and in half again and still have a readable fraction. Always list page counts in eighths (use 4/8 instead of 1/2) to more readily add and subtract the many fractions you will encounter. When the schedule changes, double–check the daily page count totals. Sometimes these totals are forgotten when it comes to recalculation. Make your primary math teacher proud.

WHY LEARN THE LANGUAGE OF THE BOARD

If time is tight, the A.D.s may hand you the board to make a one-line schedule. Know how to read (or decipher) one.

D. A.D. BREAKDOWN PAGES

Aside from the board, the Assistant Directors make a breakdown page for each scene. They thoroughly read the script and note in the large boxes on these pages what is required to be on set in order to complete each scene, from props to stunts, to Extras, to anything else. This is the information that you will use to create a shooting schedule and then, finally, the call sheets. If the A.D.s do not print the shooting schedule themselves, they will give you a copy of the breakdown pages in shooting order. They are very obvious forms to read and from which to create a shooting schedule. (See a sample in the Appendix)

E. ONE-LINE SCHEDULE

If you have to create a one-line schedule from the A.D.'s information, think that each line equals one scene and you will have a "one-liner."

WHY MAKE A ONE-LINER

Depending on the speed of production, this schedule sometimes is not created, and you will go straight to making a shooting schedule. The one-line schedule is good to display the scene order (with minimum necessary description) of the entire shooting schedule in the shortest possible format. Because it is brief, more of the crew will likely read it and all its revisions in detail.

WHAT TO PUT ON A ONE-LINER

For each scene on the one-liner, include the scene number, and scene location description. Specify day or night, the continuity day number, list of characters in that scene (by number code), page count, and the shooting location. Also include a legend to explain the number codes you used. Revise the schedule on colored paper, just like you would a script revision. The following page has a sample of a one-line schedule.

F. SHOOTING SCHEDULE

If you have to create a shooting schedule from the A.D.'s information, show all the same information as the one-line schedule, then add the detail that exists on each breakdown sheet. Include the microscene action descriptions, the various departmental set requirements, and list the character names next to the code numbers. Depending on the detail, this schedule can become almost as thick as the script in number of pages. Revise it like a script, even page by page if necessary. The following page has a sample shooting schedule. It is one of many formats you may design to suit you and the A.D. team.

SAMPLE ONE–LINE SCHEDULE

```
                    "Script Revision Nightmare"          Blue Revised
                       One-Line Schedule            Date: 9 Dec 2001

Sc#    Description                D/N   Cast           Pages         Loc

DAY 1 - TUE. JAN. 03, 2002                      1.=STUDIO, 2.=123 MAIN ST
24     INT COORDINATOR OFFICE     N2    1,3,X          1 4/8         1.
13     INT COORDINATOR OFFICE     N1    1,3            1 0/8         1.
             * * * * * * U N I T   M O V E * * * * * *
3      EXT HOUSE                   D1    1,X             1/8         2.
                       END DAY ONE - 2 5/8 PAGES

Characters
1. Coordinator (Terry)
2. Friend
3. Compy The Computer (Voice)
X  Extras
```

SAMPLE SHOOTING SCHEDULE

```
              "Script Revision Nightmare"        Pink Revised
                  Shooting Schedule          Date: 11 Dec 2001
```

DAY 1 - TUE. JAN. 03, 2002
LOC.#1 - STUDIO - 111 FILM ST.

24	INT COORDINATOR OFFICE	N2	1 4/8	1.TERRY	Props: Pens, Pencils,
	Terry breaks a window			3.COMPY	Compy Computer, Rock
				EXTRAS	to throw
				Passersby	SPFX: Breakaway window
				x2	Lighting: Streetlights
					outside visible
					Music: Radio gets
					turned off

13	INT COORDINATOR OFFICE	N1	1 0/8	1.TERRY	Props: Pens, Pencils,
	Working late at night			3.COMPY	Compy Computer
					Sound:Fax machine bell

---

* * * UNIT MOVE TO LOC.#2 - 123 MAIN ST. * * *

3	EXT HOUSE	D1	1/8	1.TERRY	Props: Misc. letters,
	Terry goes home			EXTRAS	Letter from friend
				Man with	Sets: Mailbox
				dog x1	H/M/W: Terry looks
					haggard

END DAY ONE - 2 5/8 PAGES

G. SCHEDULING FOR LOW BUDGET PRODUCTIONS

If the production is very low budget, you will not want to publish a revised, thick shooting schedule over and over again, every time there is a small schedule order change. Instead, make a "shooting schedule" (complete with all the set requirements) in script order and call it the "script breakdown." Now you are free to revise the much shorter one-line schedule every time there is a schedule change, and only revise the script breakdown when the set requirements change.

171

H. SPECIALITY BREAKDOWNS MEMOS

- List of Extras (what scene they are in, what day they play)
- List of stunts (who plays them, what day they play)
- List of picture vehicles (what day they play)
- List of... (whatever else the A.D.s think of!)

With your knowledge of schedules now, you and the Assistant Directors are a team. You can schedule anything, and you can add eighths of pages blindfolded. You are ready to make call sheets.

For the Crew Only

Few executives read all the credits in the memos you generate. They have very little time to worry about anything beyond the contractual and financing credits. It's up to you to check most of the names and spellings on your own. That is, until the credits hit the screen. I learned this when the Production Secretary and I decided to put our nick names on a very early draft of the credits.

Working on a French co-production, the Production Secretary decided that her name and mine were not in keeping with the French flare of the show. We needed appropriate nicknames. We included these names on an early draft of the credits. The Production Manager and Producer chuckled but didn't oppose the inclusion, so the credits went forward.

Executive Producers and financing companies on both sides of the Atlantic reviewed draft after draft of the credits. No one changed or deleted our "French" names. We were thrilled that all the Executives supported the little fun we injected into the credits.

Then came the first crew screening of the film. It was a heavy, dramatic film. At its inevitable conclusion, the credits began to roll. The crew was suitably depressed until the office staff credits rolled by. Chuckles and lightness filled the room. The Production Coordinator was credited as "Miss Paté" and the Production Secretary as "Babette."

A memo came to the office from the Executives the next day to remove our nicknames from the credits. Well, at least we got to see them once on screen.

YOUR NAME IN LIGHTS

Credits

You start gathering information for them in prep, make a first draft of them on first day of shooting, and end your last day in wrap trying to finalize them. They are the screen credits.

A. THE PREVIEW DRAFTS

The notes you have collected in your desk file folder about credits will be useful now. On or near day one of principal photography, make a preview draft of the credits to review with the Production Manager and Producer only. You need their input before distributing the draft to the many other people necessary because credits are a sensitive issue. It is very easy to offend someone through omission, incorrect title and/or placement, or incorrect spelling. The Production Manager and the Producer are your double checks in presenting an excellent first draft of credits. Even though contracted promises and name spellings were fresh in your mind so early in production, triple–check the promises and spellings. Be accurate from the very first preview draft.

1. Make A List of Credit Promises
To begin the preview draft, consolidate your notes to make a list of who and what credits have been promised in all contracts, deal memos, and letters of agreement. Ask the Post–Production and Legal Departments for credit promises in contracts or agreements that you do not handle.

2. Approve A Credit List Format
The Producer may have a preferred format for the credits, or may want to choose from several formats that you present. When making a format, find out as much as possible from the Producer. Which positions require a head credit? Is there a limited number of head credit cards? What positions begin the tail credits? Will the tail credits be a crawl or on cards? Ask

Post–Production how many lines can fit on a card leaving the names still legible. Watch feature films and television movies and write down the template of their credits. You will find that productions vary greatly in style. (See two samples of credit templates in the Appendix.)

3. CHECK SPELLING

Checking spelling cannot be stressed enough. Double–check! Triple–check! Be absolutely certain that everyone's name is spelled correctly. Call the Actors' Agents and confirm again how to spell each Actor's name. No computer spell check program can check the spellings of names.

4. MAKE THE FIRST PREVIEW DRAFT

Combine the information and format to create a first preview draft. The Production Manager and Producer may revise this draft several times before allowing it to be called the "first" draft for presentation to the countless Executives and companies involved in approvals. They are also relying on you to present the credits in accordance with contracted promises. Note each contracted promise in the far right margin in brackets. Since few will read all the contracts and deal memos you do, this will be a critical reference when they want to change certain credits. Here is an example:

Card #1   starring

      MO PATZ as "Terry"   ("starring," single card)

Card #2   and

      LAURA FISHER as "Compy's Voice" ("and," head credits)

5. WHO RECEIVES THE PREVIEW DRAFTS

After the Production Manager and Producer input, you may be up to the second or third preview draft. They may suggest that other people receive these "pre-first draft" credits for input. Ask if the Post–Production or the Legal Department should get copies. Mark the draft clearly that this is only a preview draft.

B. THE EARLY DRAFTS

Now that the first round of information has been collected, make the first draft of the credits.

1. Make A Cover Page Memo

Mark clearly on a cover page memo to whom these credits are going, and which draft it is. The cover page memo is designed to maintain the confidentiality of the credits underneath, and to keep track clearly of who is giving input to these credits.

2. Who Gets The Early Drafts

The first and early drafts are sent to Executives and companies for approvals. These people include all Producers, the Legal Department, Post–Production, and anyone else the Production Manager and Producer may choose. Guild and unions need to approve credits specific to their crew. Though you may not want to send them an entire draft, you can lift appropriate sections of the credits for them with a letter.

3. Call For And Record Approvals or Requests For Changes

Everyone on the cover page memo must respond to the credits with approvals or requests for changes. If some of them do not respond, call for the information. Note all changes on your copy of the credits, and code each request to the person requesting. Some requests will be in direct opposition to others. When the Producer reviews all these requests together, he/she can identify who is asking for what, and can resolve the conflict accordingly.

4. When People Change The Spelling of Their Own Names

Some people will ask for different spellings of their name to the ones contracted. If this occurs, confirm each new request in a letter or memo to that person, with a copy sent to the Producer and the Legal Department. If that person changes his/her mind after the credits are completed, you (and the Legal Department) will have written proof of the credit requested.

5. How Many Early Drafts Does It Take?

It takes many, many drafts to approve credits. The more Executives involved, the more drafts it will take. This is why you need to start the credits process as early as possible in production. When it seems to you and the Producer that the credits are approved from all sources, you are ready to make the first "final" draft.

C. THE FINAL DRAFTS

The heading reads "drafts" for a reason. As soon as you publish a final draft of the credits, someone is bound to call you with a change. Put off finalizing the credits until the last possible moment. Post Production will be able to tell you the date the credits are typeset, and then go to camera. Find out your last possible date from them.

1. Who Gets The Final Credits

Final credits go to the same people as the earlier drafts, but also to government agencies, financing agencies, publicity departments, distributors, broadcasters, and to other people that the Producer or Production Manager advises. (See a suggested list for the distribution of final credits in Chapter 18 "The Joy Of Distribution.")

2. Date The Final Drafts

Note the words "final draft" along with the date on the cover page memo and on the credits themselves. When there are several final drafts published, this will be the only way to discern them from each other. If not, revised final drafts will have to be labeled creatively, like "revised final draft," then "final and approved draft," and finally "very revised final draft."

3. Keep Post-Production Informed

Especially if there are several final drafts, keep in touch with Post–Production. Make sure they typeset and go to camera with the latest final draft of the credits. Warn them, even by telephone, when you know changes are going to be made to the credits.

Your eyes will grow tired of looking at the same names over and over again. Have an Assistant help you by double-checking the names. You will get no thanks for correctly spelling each person's name in the credits, but you will certainly hear about the one name you misspelled and forgot to check. Any oversight you make will be displayed brilliantly on the big (or little) screen. Do everything you can to be letter–perfect.

Back to Basics

As technology advances, one forgets its origins.

One show I worked on had no money to rent computers, so my office equipment consisted of a typewriter. It also had no money for a typing table, so I sat on a telephone book to get the right angle for typing.

When it came to revising the scene order on the shooting schedule, I stared in wonder at the pages, wondering how to do the job. Without a computer and without retyping, how does one revise the information and get it out to the crew quickly? I was baffled. And then it hit me — scissors and tape! I cut each scene into strips and retaped them into the correct order. How primitive, I thought, and after several revisions, this job could get really messy. But then it occurred to me, this is exactly why a computer calls its function "cut and paste."

THE JOY OF DISTRIBUTION

Tracking Paper Distribution

You know how to generate paper. You know how to hand out paper. But who got which version of which paperwork when and how? Your memory alone cannot retain such information. To make paperwork distribution a joy, you need a system to track all of the paperwork you circulate.

A. TRACKING SYSTEM

Setting up a tracking system for paperwork may seem insignificant at first, but as production proceeds, copious amounts of paperwork and revised paperwork must be distributed to a growing list of recipients, both on the crew and in offices around the world. At any given time, you must be able to know who has what information. A tracking system is essential.

1. Who Keeps Track Of Distribution

Though the job of keeping the records is often delegated to the Production Secretary, the Coordinator is ultimately responsible for the working of the system. Work together.

2. How To Make A Tracking System

You need a system that is quick and simple to update, and is easy to read by anyone. Here are two different systems that work well:

PAPER DISTRIBUTION BINDER

Devote one binder to paper distribution. Use divider tabs to mark the differing types of paperwork (each episode script, crew list, cast list, call sheet, etc.). In each section create a chart that lists the names of the people or companies to receive this paperwork in the first column, and mark the rest of the columns for each revision of that paperwork, labeling color and date. When distributing the paperwork to each recipient, note in each appropriate box the date of sending. You can also use codes to note the method used, like "D" for delivered, "F" for faxed, and "C" for couriered.

SCRIPT #1	White-Dec.1	Pink-Dec.2	Blue-Dec.
Parent Company	C-Dec.1	C-Dec.2	C-Dec.3
Clearance Company	C-Dec.2		
Production Manager	D-Dec.1	D-Dec.2	D-Dec.3
Casting Director	F-Dec.1		
etc.			

CHARTS ON WALL ENVELOPES

Remembering you have wall envelopes collecting paperwork for various companies, you can create a chart to post on each one to use as your tracking system. List the paperwork that company requires in the first column, and mark the rest of the columns with each revision of that paperwork, labeling color only. When delivering the contents of the envelopes, note the date in each appropriate box. Though this system shows you at a glance which paperwork each company receives, not every company you will distribute to has a wall envelope. For those without wall envelopes, keep a written log elsewhere.Crew List

PARENT COMPANY	White	Pink	Blue
Script #1	C-Dec.1	C-Dec.2	C-Dec3
Crew List	C-Dec.2		
Cast List #1	C-Dec.2		
Call sheet Ep.#1	F-Dec.5		
etc.			

3. Keep Extra Copies of Paperwork On Standby

You will discover very quickly that some people have a natural tendency to lose paperwork over and over again. Other people will take the last copy from the distribution table and not inform you. Especially keep an extra copy or two of collated fully colored scripts on standby (but not on the distribution table) for these purposes. You will welcome the standby copies when you are rushed and have to generate a collated seven-colored script for someone immediately.

4. Two Collated Scripts In Office For Sides

Besides any standby copies of the script, keep two fully collated scripts in the office for use when making the daily sides for the set. At the end of the production, these scripts, if well kept, can serve as master copies for any final scripts that you must photocopy for executives and companies.

5. Store Leftover Copies In An "Archive" Box

As some people tend to lose paperwork, so other people and companies will remember at a later date which paperwork they require. Keep old versions of all paperwork in an "archive" box instead of throwing them out. Often these people will be satisfied with an older copy of the script because they just want to have an idea of the plot.

B. STARTER DISTRIBUTION LISTS

The checklists that follow will jog your memory when distributing anything, paper or otherwise.

DEPARTMENT HEADS

When you have something to go to all department heads, refer to this list. When creating your own distribution lists, review this list to be sure you address the entire crew.

- •Producer (any and all)
- •Director
- •Story Editor

- Production Manager
- Production Coordinator
- Production Accountant
- 1st A.D.
- Location Manager
- Continuity Supervisor
- Casting Director
- Publicist
- Production Designer
- Art Director
- Set Decorator
- Property Master
- Wardrobe Designer
- Hair Stylist
- Makeup Artist
- Director of Photography
- Sound Mixer
- Key Grip
- Gaffer
- Special Effects Supervisor
- Stunt Coordinator
- Construction Manager
- Transportation Coordinator
- Post-Production Supervisor

OFFICE KEYS LIST

As a preliminary list, use this checklist to start your key list. Review the names with the Production Manager. Do not just copy tons of keys and hand them out. Use a sign-out list. Know who will actually be using the office after hours. If you have an alarm system, make sure each person with a key knows how to use it properly.

- Producer
- Production Manager
- Production Coordinator
- Production Secretary
- Office Production Assistant
- 1st A.D.
- 2nd A.D.
- 3rd A.D.
- Location Manager
- Location Scout
- Production Designer
- Art Director
- Set Decorator
- Property Master
- Wardrobe Designer
- Construction Manager
- Transportation Coordinator
- Driver Captain
- Head Driver
- Craft Service

C. THE JOY OF DISTRIBUTION LISTS

It is time to move onto the majority of the paperwork distribution lists you will require. Examine and fine–tune these lists with the Production Manager to create your own "Joy of Distribution" lists. When completed, give copies of your lists to all the office staff, and to the A.D.s (for set-related distribution).

1. Script–Related Paperwork
Scripts are generally very long documents; therefore keep an accurate list of who receives each script to prevent excessive photocopying.

SCRIPT — EARLY DRAFTS

If the draft is very early in pre-production some of the people on this list may not be hired yet. Even though the list of names is long, check with the Producer which of these people really need to receive the current early draft of the script.

- •Script Research Company
- •Executive Producer
- •Producer
- •Director
- •Story Editor
- •Casting Director
- •Director of Photography
- •Production Manager
- •Production Coordinator
- •Production Designer
- •1st A.D.
- •2nd A.D.
- •Location Manager
- •Art Director

- Set Decorator
- Property Master
- Wardrobe Designer
- Continuity Supervisor
- Sound Mixer
- Gaffer
- Key Grip
- Special Effects Supervisor
- Stunt Coordinator
- Transportation Coordinator

SCRIPT — MAJOR REVISIONS ONLY

This distribution list is for those who do not need every little revision of the script.

- Publicist
- Performers Unions
- Government Agencies

SCRIPT — EVERY REVISION

At this point, it is too obvious to list the entire shooting crew on this list. These are recipients not on the set to also consider.

- Distributor or Broadcaster
- Funding Agencies
- Executive Producer & Head Office Personnel
- Editors
- Completion Bond Company

SCRIPT RESEARCH REPORT

The clearance company responds with notes of character names that must change, songs that must be cleared before singing on set, and warnings of any copyrights and trademarks that are being infringed. (See more on clearances in Chapter 20, "It's Clear To Me Now.") Distribute this report to:

- Executive Producer
- Producer
- Director
- Story Editor
- Legal Department
- Production Manager
- Production Coordinator
- Production Accountant
- 1st A.D.
- Production Designer
- Art Director
- Set Decorator
- Wardrobe Designer
- Continuity Supervisor

2. Schedule-Related Paperwork

You are already familiar with numerous kinds of schedules. Besides the crew, these are other people to keep informed. Call them to confirm which paperwork they require.

CALL SHEET (SENT VIA FAX DAILY)

- Distributor or Broadcaster
- Performers Unions

- Crew Unions
- Extras Casting Director
- Funding Agencies
- Government Agencies
- Completion Bond Company

ONE-LINE SCHEDULE & PRODUCTION SCHEDULE

- Executive Producer & Head Office
- Editors
- Publicist
- Distributor or Broadcaster
- Funding Agencies
- Government Agencies
- Completion Bond Company

SHOOTING SCHEDULE

- Executive Producer & Head Office
- Editors
- Publicist
- Performers Unions
- Funding Agencies
- Government Agencies
- Completion Bond Company
- Actors (who are not on set)

3. Other Paperwork
This section is made up of lists, contracts, and breakdowns. Since you, as the Coordinator, are responsible to disseminate information to those not on the crew, these lists cover only those people and companies.

CREW LIST

- Executive Producer & Head Office
- Editors
- Publicist
- Distributor or Broadcaster
- Crew Unions
- Performers Unions
- Funding Agencies
- Government Agencies
- Completion Bond Company

CAST LIST

- Executive Producer & Head Office
- Editors
- Publicist
- Distributor or Broadcaster
- Performers Unions
- Funding Agencies
- Government Agencies
- Completion Bond Company

PERFORMER CONTRACTS

- •Talent Agent for Performer
- •Production Accountant
- •Production Coordinator
- •Legal Department
- •A.D. (with pay rates masked)

PERFORMERS' PICTURE & RESUMES

- •Production Coordinator
- •Publicist
- •Wardrobe & Hair/Makeup Departments

EXTRAS BREAKDOWN MEMO

- •Performers Union
- •Extras Casting Director
- •Executive Producer & Head Office
- •Production Coordinator

CREDIT LIST — FINAL

- •Executive Producer & Head Office
- •Producer
- •Legal Department
- •Production Manager
- •Production Coordinator
- •Production Accountant

- Publicist
- Post–Production Supervisor
- Distributor or Broadcaster
- Funding Agencies
- Government Agencies
- Completion Bond Company

D. THE PRODUCTION REPORT and ALL ITS BACKUP LISTS

As you know, the daily production report is actually a compilation of reports from each of the departments. Each departmental report has its own set of recipients as does the production report. Start with these distribution lists, consult each department and the Production Manager, and create your own set of report distribution lists for the production. Determine and note who keeps the original of each report.

PRODUCTION REPORT — DRAFT COPY

Be sure the Production Manager has approved even the draft copy before distributing this document.

- Production Accountant
- A.D. (who writes the report on set)
- Executive Producer
- Completion Bond Company
- Production Coordinator

PRODUCTION REPORT — TYPED & SIGNED COPY

Now approved by all parties, the production report has a wider distribution. It remains a confidential report. Treat it as such.

- Production Coordinator (keep the original)
- Executive Producer
- Producer
- Production Manager
- Production Accountant
- 1st A.D.
- A.D. (who write the report on set)
- Funding Agencies
- Completion Bond Company

CONTINUITY TOP SHEET

This report is the Continuity Supervisor's summary of all scenes shot or not, and an update on the timing of the entire script. This is the form to refer to when completing the continuity section of the production report.

- Continuity Supervisor
- Editors
- Executive Producer
- Producer
- Production Manager
- Production Coordinator

OTHER CONTINUITY PAPERWORK

Shot reports, log forms, wild sound reports, and any other continuity paperwork detail even further for the editors all the information they need to know for post–production.

- Continuity Supervisor

- Editors
- Production Coordinator

SOUND REPORT SHEETS

The Sound Department reports on the quality of the contents of each roll of sound stock they use. They usually use a two-part form that enables them to keep a copy of their paperwork upon sending you the editing copy. These are the forms you count when completing the sound stock used section of the production report.

- Editors
- Production Coordinator

CAMERA REPORTS

Just like the Sound Department, the Camera Department reports to the lab and the Editors the contents of each roll of film. The circled numbers indicate to the lab which takes to print, so that they do not go to the expense of printing the already-identified bad takes.

- Editors
- Production Coordinator

DAILY FILM STOCK SUMMARY

The Camera Department also reports to production the amount of film used to date, and the amount of unused film on hand. This is the form to refer to when completing the film totals section of the production report.

- Production Coordinator

PERFORMER WORK REPORTS

Already discussed, this form is essentially a time sheet for Actors. Refer to it when completing the performer's section of the production report.

- Production Accountant
- Performers Union
- Production Coordinator

EXTRAS VOUCHERS

These forms serve as both contracts for Extras, and time sheets. Refer to these when completing the extras section of the production report.

- Production Accountant
- Performers Union
- Production Coordinator

DRIVER TIMES

Since the Transportation Department often wraps at the end of the day after the last A.D., they forward their daily work times into the office later. Sometimes you have to call for this information. These timings will complete the crew attendance section on the production report.

- Transportation Coordinator
- Production Accountant
- Production Coordinator

You have noticed that you keep a copy of every piece of paper you distribute. Paperwork gets lost now and then. You have the backup copy for anything you or the office handles. And now that you have a record of everything that has been distributed through the office, you discover the "joy" is back in the joy of paper distribution.

SPECIAL ISSUES

The Box At Customs

When it comes to shipping props, you can ship an incredibly wide variety of items. You have to know how to handle each one separately when it comes to customs clearances. One word missing can stop a shipment and delay a shoot.

On one show, we had to ship crates and crates of props to New Zealand for a period piece. All parts of the paperwork were carefully reviewed over and over again for accuracy and completeness. At the border one crate stopped dead.

Customs refused to open the case to examine the contents. They asked the shipper present if the contents were real or fake, since the documents did not specify. The shipper too refused to open the case to find out. They telephoned me back home to ask if I had forgotten to include the word "fake" on this contents list. I asked them to be more specific. They said they refused to open the case to find out; they just wanted my answer, and read to me the list of contents.

I held back my laughter and apologized for the oversight and insisted that yes, the props were indeed fake. The two items that had concerned them so deeply were one human ear and one baby's head!

CROSSING THE BORDER

Couriers and Customs

When production decides that there is a very special item for set that needs to be imported from another country, you know you cannot ship it as easily as you can across town. Knowing also that the item is required on set in a day or two, it is time to make friends with a customs broker.

A. COURIERS (LOCAL AND INTERNATIONAL)

You have set up accounts with both local and international couriers. You are comfortable with their services because you can call them after hours, they are quick to respond, and they are reasonably affordable. They have preprinted your company name on a series of waybills. There is a bit more you should know.

FILL OUT WAYBILLS COMPLETELY

Whether local or international, get into the habit of filling out each waybill completely. If you think that packages are delivered without a telephone number, the date, or a complete description of the contents, you are right most of the time. Realize, however, that noting the telephone number aids the courier if he/she cannot find the address or person; noting the date and contents aids you if someone forgets to enter the information into the distribution binder. Completing waybills only helps you.

LOG OR KEEP WAYBILLS

Use a log form to record each couriered envelope or package. You will refer to this log. You send a lot of packages to numerous people and companies. Your memory cannot retain the information. Your memory cannot help you when you have to trace lost packages.

KNOW YOUR COURIER'S SERVICES

Know when the last pickup is for your courier. Know where the drop boxes are and those last pickup times. Know what is the last time you can take a package to their airport location and still get the package out that night. Due to the nature of the film industry, you will almost always be working on those last–minute times.

TAXIS AS LOCAL COURIERS

Taxis deliver people or packages in town. They can be faster than the fastest service your courier can provide, but they tend to be more expensive. Taxi companies can set you up with an account and give you chits to fill out instead of handling cash. They charge an administration fee on top of the price of each ride for this convenience.

THE EFFICIENT OFFICE P.A.

If you have an efficient Office Production Assistant, you will find you do not need your local courier very often. An Office P.A. who knows the city and can manage time will cut your courier bill down to minimum. He/she is also equipped with more knowledge about production, and therefore production's priorities, than any courier or taxi driver. Use this to your advantage.

B. CUSTOMS BROKER

Documents easily cross borders, bypassing customs. Working for a film company, you will rarely be shipping only documents. There are many restrictions and many forms for items that have to pass through customs to enter your country. You need a customs broker to help you.

POWER OF AUTHORITY LETTER

When you have chosen a customs broker to work for you, produce a letter addressed to that broker giving him/her the power of authority to clear packages through customs for you. It is a very short letter that can read like this:

> Customs Broker
>
> Customs Broker Address
>
> To whom it may concern:

This letter authorizes (customs broker company) to act on behalf of FILM COMPANY INC. ("FILM TITLE") relating to all customs clearances.

COURIERS KNOW SIMPLE CUSTOMS PAPERWORK

International couriers know about the customs paperwork to be completed for many shipments. If you ask, they will supply you with appropriate forms and directions for the do-it-yourself approach. Use this approach for repeated simple packages, like the daily videotapes you may be shipping. If you are ever concerned about the correct paperwork or customs procedure, call your customs broker for advice.

C. VIDEOTAPES CROSSING BORDERS

Rushes, rough cuts, and delivered shows may have you shipping your share of videotapes across international borders. Confirm with the courier or broker that no more paperwork is needed than a commercial invoice and a videotape declaration to accompany the waybill. The commercial invoice describes in more detail what the waybill explains, and the videotape declaration is your assurance that the videotapes do not contain material that is pornographic or treason.

COMMERCIAL INVOICE — SMALL SHIPMENTS

The waybill often has a section that is called "Commercial Invoice." Completing this section is sufficient for international videotape shipments except for very large shipments. Note how many videotapes and which format are in the package, then mark in large letters in this section that the tapes are "FOR REFERENCE ONLY; NOT FOR RESALE." Assuming you are sending rushes or cut shows for approvals, "for reference" is what they are.

COMMERCIAL INVOICE — LARGE SHIPMENTS

For large shipments, make a secondary, more detailed commercial invoice on letterhead, as shown here.

(Letterhead)

Date of shipment

To Whom: (name, address, phone, fax)

Description of Contents: (i.e., one VHS videotape)

Value of Contents: (note value and currency)

Reason for Export: (i.e., Daily rushes of "Film" for reference only; not for resale)

How Shipped: (courier company name & waybill number)

Signed (your name & title)

VIDEOTAPE/FILM DECLARATION

If you cannot get a form from the courier or broker, make one on letter-head like this:

(Letterhead)

Date of shipment

To Whom: (name, address, phone, fax)

Waybill Number

Description of Contents: (i.e., one VHS videotape)

Length of Videotape or Film: (i.e., 30 minutes)

Reason for Export: (i.e., Daily rushes of "Film" for reference only; not for resale)

I/we declare that the FILM(S)/VIDEO(S) contain no obscene or immoral matter, nor any matter advocating or urging treason or insurrection against (country of destination), nor any threat to take the life of, or inflict bodily harm upon any person in (country of destination).

Signed (your name & title)

D. WARDROBE CROSSING BORDERS

Imagine sending a knife wrapped in a T-shirt (for safety) from one country to another, complete with customs documents for the knife. You may wonder why the package stops at customs. Customs will be looking for the proper documentation for the T-shirt. They need to know what the article of clothing is, its value, why you are shipping it, what fiber makes up the fabric, and where each of those fibers were made in the world. Each piece of information requires a separate form. When you ship clothing, you need the help of your customs broker.

REQUEST FOR REDUCTION OF DUTY LETTER

When you courier large shipments of wardrobe internationally, large duty and taxes are triggered because customs assumes the wardrobe is arriving to stay. To apply for reduction of these duties and taxes, because production is only renting the wardrobe, draft a letter with the help of your broker (who will know the latest procedure) to the customs office. Start with the following draft letter, customizing the information to your production.

(Letterhead)

Date

Collector

Customs Office

Dear sir:

Please consider this letter an application for reduction of duty and taxes for the wardrobe (see attached lists). I am applying on behalf of the importer, FILM COMPANY, INC., whose address is listed here. We are a (country of nationality) crew currently in production of a (type of film) entitled "FILM

TITLE" for (note where it will be distributed or broadcast). Below please find our responses to the questions regarding responsibility of the importer:

a) *Name and address of importer:*

(film company's name & address)

b) *Contact within company:*

(Production Coordinator's name, head of Wardrobe's name)

c) *Financial Hardship:*

We believe that full duty and taxes would be excessive considering the short period of time that the wardrobe will be in the country. These goods are obtainable only from the (country of export) and will be returned immediately.

d) *Why are goods required:*

We are filming "FILM TITLE" that requires authentic (describe originality of wardrobe).

e) *Goods not available from national suppliers:*

The above mentioned goods could not be obtained from the top costume houses in (your country) due to their peculiarity within the time and budget allotted.

f) *List of companies and persons contacted:*

(Name at least three companies you contacted for this wardrobe. Include letters from these companies reporting that they do not have this particular wardrobe.)

g) "Public Interest":

This production employs many people from the shooting crew to the support industries, such as (note appropriate suppliers you use, like equipment houses, hotels, restaurants, airlines, limousines, post-production laboratories and sound facilities, telephone systems, studio rentals, the unions and guilds, etc.). If we cannot obtain the goods within the required time and budget, we will have to shut down production until such time as we can have appropriate wardrobe made for filming, which would mean a shutdown of at least (mention an estimated time frame). This shutdown will effect an excess of (number of employees) people with a loss of income.

h) Statement:

See attached letter from Production Manager (the letter is described below).

i) National Competitors:

We have contacted everyone possible to obtain the required costumes and they are unable to provide the goods. Nor can anyone suggest anyone in (your country) that can.

j) Any objections to reveal company's name:

Film Company, Inc., does not have any objections to its name being revealed.

k) Description of what makes them special in nature:

(describe the costumes)

l) Use of goods:

As wardrobe for a (feature film or television movie).

m) Where goods are to be used:

"FILM TITLE" movie currently filming in (city).

n) Value of goods:

(note overall value and currency)

o) Estimated date of arrival:

Shipment from (costume company name) in (city, country) on (date of arrival).

If you require further information, I can be reached at the production number listed below. I look forward to hearing from you in the near future.

Signed (your name and title)

WARDROBE SUPPLIER LETTERS (Item f.)

The head of Wardrobe will usually arrange for these letters for you. If the supplier asks you to draft the wording, since they are busy, start with the following:

"Film Company, Inc., has requested the rental of (specify costumes). We do not have such costumes in our stock and do not know of another company in (your country) that can assist them with this rental."

STATEMENT LETTER (Item h.)

Create and attach a letter to customs from the Production Manager that promises the film company will cover all duty and taxes should the request for reduction of duty be denied. Begin with the following wording:

"This letter is to confirm that FILM COMPANY, INC., would accept responsibility of payment in full of duties and taxes applicable under the (appropriate tax act), if the request for reduction of duty and taxes is not approved."

COMMERCIAL INVOICE

Type up a commercial invoice on letterhead, just as you do for video-tapes, detailing exactly the items that are being imported. The costume company will have a detailed list since they have to generate one for rental and accounting purposes anyway. Do not simply photocopy their forms (which you will also use for customs). Make the commercial invoice easy to read, listing the items clearly, and noting the overall value rather than individual values.

E. FILM EQUIPMENT CROSSING BORDERS

If you take film equipment to certain countries for the filming period and return with it, your customs broker will help you to obtain a carnet. This document lists every single item of film equipment (right down to each filter), all serial numbers, every value, and promises that this equipment will be in the country only temporarily. This is a complex form to get. Use your customs broker.

F. OTHER ITEMS CROSSING BORDERS

You can ship almost anything: contact lenses, animals, props, antiques, and so on. Since countries have different restrictions and requirements for

205

each shipment, contact your customs broker for the latest procedures for each shipment.

G. HAND–CARRYING ITEMS ACROSS BORDERS

Due to time constraints, sometimes the only remaining alternative is to fly a person across a border to hand–carry the item to its destination. Because this is a last resort method of shipping, any delay at the border is critical. Paperwork must be perfectly complete and accurate. Review all the paperwork necessary with the customs broker. The broker may arrange for someone at the airport to aid you through customs. Along with all that paperwork, give a letter of identification to the person hand–carrying the package.

(Letterhead)

Date

To whom it may concern:

(Person's name) is hand-carrying (describe item) for the film entitled "FILM TITLE." (Describe reason for the export and if the item is being returned to the country.)

The value of (the item) for customs purposes is: (amount and currency).

Signed (your name and title)

As you grow accustomed to foreign shipments, you will be amazed by how similar the various customs forms actually are. Each one requires so much of the same information over and over again with one or two extra items. You may never stop being amazed, but you will soon learn what forms are appropriate to which packages, and astound the crew on your knowledge of customs.

Sing to Me in Public Domain

Actors often invent unscripted business on set for their characters, to add depth and personality to their performances. That's wonderful, unless the unscripted business is singing unscripted, copyrighted songs.

One Actor I worked with had this tendency, and the first two songs did not prove to be a big problem. After watching the rushes, I arranged for licenses to use the songs that he sang. Both licenses were reasonable. Twice lucky. But the third song...

Watching the rushes, I was relieved that the actor had chosen to hum a piece of his own making. It was a totally unintelligible, nonsense collection of sounds. Not so, apparently.

The day before broadcast, the Production Secretary was dubbing a copy of the show and commented how long it has been since she's heard that song. "Song?" I asked. She told me the title and artist. It was no collection of sounds, as I originally thought; it was an obscure, old, and still copyrighted song.

The Producer asked me to get a quote on the license. I discovered a catch. The particular broadcaster airing our show was not signatory with the performing rights company that covered the song. The performing rights company did not want to grant a license at any cost. They wanted the broadcaster to become signatory.

So, to this day, Lawyers speak with Lawyers about this song, and the particular Actor was never allowed to sing or hum unscripted songs on set again, unless it could be proven before call time that the songs were indeed in the public domain.

IT'S CLEAR TO ME NOW

Rights and Clearances

Sometimes the Producer does it. Sometimes the Legal Department does it. Often you will do it. "It" is the clearing of rights to copyrighted works, like songs or photographs, for use in a film production. This chapter cannot be an exhaustive description of legal rights and clearances, and does not intend to be such. It will help you to embark on another facet of film making. Keep in constant contact with the Legal Department for advice as you enter the world of rights and clearances.

A. THE SCRIPT CLEARANCE REPORT

Script clearance has been mentioned several times so far. Here is more information about these critical reports.

1. *How Clearance Reports Work*

If the script has a character named John Smith who is a dentist from a particular city, the clearance company will research to see if such a man exists. If there are many John Smiths in that city, and none of them are dentists, then the name "John Smith" is clear for use in the film. If, however, there is one John Smith who is a dentist in all of North America, or if there is only one John Smith in that city, then the clearance company will suggest you change the character name in the script to avoid any possible lawsuit. The real John Smith may see the film, decide that the character is a derogatory portrayal of himself, and sue. As the production company, you want to use "clear" names in the script.

2. *First Conversation With A Clearance Company*

When you first talk to the script clearance company, know where and when the script takes place. Is the film fictional or is it based on a true story? Where is the film going to be distributed or broadcast? From this information and other questions they will ask, the clearance company will determine the scope of the clearance you need, and the two of you can negotiate a price.

3. *The Clearance Company and Script Revisions*

Keep the clearance company abreast of all script revisions as soon as possible. Once you are aware of how they read a script, you can telephone in script changes as you type them, thereby giving them extra time to research the new material.

4. *The Reluctance of Changing Names*

Writers, Story Editors, and Producers may be reluctant to change names they deem trivial or absolutely essential to the story as is. Changing names is legal preventative medicine, so involve the Legal Department. Together the Legal Department and Producer can evaluate the potential legal risk and come up with a decision to change the names or not.

5. *Addressing the Suggestions on the Clearance Report*

After distributing the clearance report, read it carefully, and ensure that each suggestion for change is addressed by the production team.

CHARACTER NAMES THAT DO NOT CLEAR

Have the Writers or Story Editor generate a list of replacement names in descending order of priority to send to the clearance company for "reclearing" immediately. Once a replacement name is cleared, send a memo to everyone who gets the clearance report, and place an extra copy in your script revision file on your desk to remind you when next revising the script. The immediacy of the memo will help the wardrobe departments, for example, build clothing labels using correct, clear names.

LOCATION NAMES THAT DO NOT CLEAR

If the script is fictitious, the names of the locations must also be fictitious (unless you have permission from those locations). If an actual location, like a restaurant, and its name is used on screen, then the script, legally, is no longer located in a fictitious place. Actual locations make the clearing of character names more complex and iffy. Get replacement names to the clearance company as soon as possible. The Art Department will likely have to build signs to identify these fictitious buildings on screen.

TRADEMARKS THAT DO NOT CLEAR

Trademarks like "Kleenex," and "Xerox" are often mentioned in scripts when what is actually meant is "facial tissue" and "photocopy." The clearance report will note these trademarks for you. If you do not change these words in the script, you must contact each company to negotiate written permission to use their trademarked name on screen. Since most corporate companies do not work at the speed of film companies, permissions can take up to six or eight weeks. For trivial on screen references, your time and effort is not worth it. Change the references.

REFERENCES THAT ALMOST DO NOT CLEAR

People who work at clearance companies seem to have seen every film ever made, read every book on the market, and speak every language in the world. These people are amazing. You may see a comment in the clearance report that notes a certain visual look is particularly like that of another film already made, or a certain phrase has been published in a book already on the market, or that a certain work or character name actually means something terribly rude in another language. Discuss these comments with the Producer and Legal Department. Find out how they will address these notes.

6. Where To Ask For Permission

You have a copyrighted or trademarked name that you really want to use in the film but you do not know whom to ask for permission. If the contact name and number are not already on the clearance report, telephone and ask the clearance company. Though they are not negotiators for you, they will find out where you have to go to seek permission.

7. Using Actual Names

Sometimes you will use names of real people or of real locations.

USING AN ACTUAL PERSON'S NAME

When the script uses the name of a person, be it a crew member or a friend, draft a short letter from that person giving the film company permission to use the name. The Legal Department needs all such permissions in writing in order to access production insurance policies for distribution. Be simple, creating the letter with wording like: "I give Film Company, Inc.,

210

permission to use my name in the film 'FILM TITLE' to be exploited in all media throughout the world in perpetuity. I understand that my name will not be used in a derogatory manner." Review the wording with the Legal Department for simplicity and full legal coverage.

USING AN ACTUAL LOCATION OR COMPANY NAME

Location agreements usually contain a clause to give the film company permission to use the company name on screen when filming there. Do not assume all location agreements do, and check this with the Location Manager. If there is no such clause and you intend to see the company's name on screen, generate a letter granting the permission you need, but first review the letter with the Legal Department.

B. MUSIC CLEARANCES

If there are a lot of songs in the script and the film company has the funds, hire a music clearance company to clear the songs for you. They will identify songs that are in the public domain (and are therefore free) and will save you from an enormous and time–consuming job. If, however, you have to (or want to) clear the music in the script, here are a few things you should know.

1. *What Is Public Domain?*

Songs in the public domain are free to use, because their copyright has expired. When the owner of the copyright has been dead for a certain length of time, his/her work is put into the public domain. The required number of years, from 50 to 100, varies from country to country. Therefore, note that a song can be in the public domain in one country, but not necessarily in another. Ask the Legal Department what age is required for your production. Be aware that there are many familiar songs that are not in the public domain. "Happy Birthday to You" is still a copyrighted work.

2. *Types of Rights*

Once you select a song to use, there are four type of rights you may need to buy before using that song.

PUBLISHING (OR SYNCHRONIZATION) RIGHTS

As the name suggests, you must contact a Music Publisher to purchase a publishing rights license. This license grants you permission to use the "sheet music" for a particular song. This license in hand, you can hum that song, sing that song, play that song, or make up your own version of that song on screen. However, note that this license is only one of two you need to play an existing recording of that song.

RECORDING RIGHTS

As the name suggests, most of the time you have to contact a Record Company to get a recording rights license. This license grants you permission to play a particular recording of a song on screen. This license does not include the Publisher's permission. You must obtain a publishing rights license separately.

ARTISTS' RIGHTS

Sometimes the Record Company does not hold all the rights to a recording, because the Artist has retained some rights. Ask the Record Company if Artists' rights are applicable to this recording. Artists' rights are negotiated through the Record Company or through the Artist's Manager.

ARRANGEMENT RIGHTS

Not all songs in the public domain are free to use. Some have arrangement rights attached to them. An Arranger can take a song in the public domain, publish his own arrangement, and copyright that arrangement. As the description suggests, it is a Publisher you will need to contact to negotiate arrangement rights.

SO, WHAT ARE MASTER RIGHTS?

You will hear the term "master rights" used frequently. "Publishing rights" are actually called "master rights." "Recording rights" are called "master recording rights" (but are often incorrectly called "master rights").

By using the terms "publishing" and "recording" instead of "master," you cannot mix up the two licenses, and people in the industry will understand you.

3. Where To Look For Rights

For publishing rights, start with a music rights agency (like the Harry Fox Agency in the U.S.A., or C.M.R.R.A. in Canada). They are authorized to negotiate licenses with film companies. Or, call the index department of the music performer rights associations (A.S.C.A.P., B.M.I., or S.O.C.A.N.) with the name of the song. Both can furnish you with the name of the Publisher, and will also know if arrangement rights apply.

For recording rights, simply refer to the CD cover for the name of the Record Company. Contact the Permissions or Legal Department and request permission. Post–Production will consider a CD an adequate source from which to duplicate the recording onto the soundtrack. If there is no CD of the song, ask the Record Company to supply you with a master of the recording.

4. Terms, Territories, Usage, Fees

When you are set to negotiate for the rights, address this criteria:

TERM

Often license fees vary for a 5-year term, 10-year term, or perpetuity. Naturally, the longer the term, the higher the price. Buy as much as you can afford. Distributors and Legal Departments love the words "in perpetuity" so that a few years from now they will not have to buy the rights all over again.

TERRITORY

You can get a license to cover one country, or pay more and cover the world. Find out from the Producer the plan for the film's distribution. Will production or distribution pay for all those foreign territories?

USAGE

Is the song to be hummed, sung, or instrumental? Is it a record playing or a band miming to the recording? Is the song atmosphere in the background or a critical part of the scene's action? Have some script pages handy to demonstrate the song's usage in the scene when you ask for permission. The owners need to know how the song is to be handled. Is it being used in a derogatory manner? Is it a parody of the work? Are new lyrics being written?

FEES

A character hums an identifiable song in the script as he walks in the door. The Producer wants to know how much the use of that song will cost. Fees vary drastically, taking into consideration the range of terms, territories and usages, the size of your production, and each particular Publisher. Each song will be different. A price quotation is time-consuming for you and the Publisher, so be sure you really want that song before you start the process of asking for permission.

5. Stock Music

Stock music is generally low-copyright music. If you are specific about a song, but not about an arrangement or performer, then you can contact a stock music supplier to find the music in their files that will do. They charge research fees, so be specific. They charge transfer fees, so be sure from Post–Production exactly which delivery format is acceptable. The license fee is sold to you at a very discounted price compared to that of the big publishers, and the license will be for use throughout the world and in perpetuity.

6. Promise of a Screen Credit

Song credits are not short. For each piece of music, count on three to four lines of text to credit any or all of the song title, the Composer, the Publisher, the Performer, and the Record Company. Be upfront with the Record Company about credits. It is standard to credit songs, but if the production is too small to warrant many credits of any kind, address this issue early. Do not wait for the license to arrive stating credits expected and specifications defined.

7. *When You Cannot Find The Owner*

Rights can change hands. They expire. They revert back to the Composers. Publishers are bought out by other Publishers. Sometimes you cannot find the rights to a song no matter how hard you try. Keep notes of everyone you contact in your search for the owner. If after a few weeks your search has still been to no avail, the Legal Department can review your notes and may decide that enough effort went into the search, and the song can be used anyway; or they may recommend removing the song.

8. *Singing Unscripted Songs On Set*

Actors can be asked to ad–lib a song on the set. Talk to the A.D.s and do not let any actor hum a song that is not in the public domain! Clearing a song after it has been cut into the film is a nearly impossible task. With the film completed, you are no longer in a bargaining position. If the owner does not want to sell you the rights, or is charging an exorbitant fee, you have no way out but to cut the offending song from the film.

9. *Cue Sheets*

Post–Production should be aware they have to forward cue sheets on to the music performer rights associations (A.S.C.A.P., B.M.I., or S.O.C.A.N.). Cue sheets report when and how many seconds of each song is played in the film. They also identify the respective owners of each song. The associations use this information to calculate royalty payments to the Composers. Read the licenses you have purchased. They may also require that a copy of the cue sheets go to the Publisher and/or Record Company. If so, send a memo to Post–Production relating this information.

C. PHOTOGRAPH CLEARANCES

When you are getting permission to use a photograph from a stock library or a magazine, note that there are two kinds of rights that may apply: "magazine rights" and "photographer rights." Treat these clearances much the same as music clearances. As the magazine is like a Publisher, the Photographer is like the Music Artist. The magazine's Legal Department will know if the Photographer has retained any rights to the photograph you wish to use. If the people depicted in the photograph are unrecognizable, there are no more rights to buy. Note, however, that if the people are recognizable, you must seek permission from each one of these people, too. A simple letter granting permission to the film company will suffice, but it is wise to discuss this situation anyway with the Legal Department before pursuing photograph clearances.

D. OTHER CLEARANCES

Rights are attached to numerous items: radio shows, posters, artwork, and so on. The script clearance report will note these copyrighted items, and lead you to the source for getting the appropriate permissions.

E. PRODUCT PLACEMENT

Product placement is when a company pays the production money to show their product or logo on screen. It is a form of advertising for the company, and a source of revenue for the production. Not all productions, however, want to advertise products in the course of telling a story. If yours does, you can approach companies directly, or contact a product placement agent in your reference books.

You have impressed the crew with your organization. You have impressed the crew with your knowledge of customs. Now you will impress the crew with your knowledge of rights and clearances. Refer to the Legal Department at any time. They will be happy to share their knowledge with you. Just be sure that you have all the necessary rights before committing anything to screen.

WRAP

Who's in Charge?

Though the hierarchy of a film production deems the Executive Producer most in charge, that is not true all of the time. At the wrap party, the Coordinator rules.

For one wrap party, we rented a cruising boat to tour the harbor. On the several decks we were supplied with a wonderful buffet, danceable music, and incredible views of the city. The party was a great success, and the Executive Producer, along with the Producer and Production Manager, decided that it should continue for another hour. The Executive Producer was willing to cover the expense on his own credit card.

The boat crew refused them their request. They needed the permission of a woman named Deborah. This must be the boat's manager, the producing trio assumed. And a search went out for this Deborah. When she was found, she was escorted to the scene of the request.

The Executive Producer, Producer, and Production Manager were rather surprised to find out that the person who appeared was not the boat's manager, but rather their own Production Coordinator. In front of the trio, the boat crew asked Deborah for permission to extend the party. I quickly said "Yes, of course!", and then turned to the Executive Producer: "Sir, you have my approval to spend your own money."

IT'S A WRAP

Wrapping Up Production

The last day of principal photography is here. Crew members are talking about their next jobs. Your mind is concerned with the last phase of coordinating this show. Tomorrow you start the first day of wrap. It is time to empty the entire office again. It is time to arrange a celebratory party.

A. EMPTYING THE OFFICE

In wrap you must return everything that you rented, sell everything that you bought, and pack up all the files for head office storage. Since Chapter 2 ("The Big Setup") lists all the items you arranged, such a list will not be repeated here. Review and reverse that chapter. There are, however, further issues to address in tying up production into a neat wrap package.

1. Report to the Wrap File
You already have a file in the cabinet called "wrap." In this file, keep all the memos and copies of letters reporting what happened to everything (from furniture to the linen delivery) at the end of the film.

2. The Inventory List
Back in pre-production you created an inventory list (or kept a detailed P.O. log) of everything that you bought and rented as it happened. This list is invaluable to you now to double–check that all items indeed get wrapped. Much time has elapsed since the beginning of pre-production, and your memory will need the assistance.

3. Make a Summary Memo of Return Items and Ongoing Issues
As you return items (from walkie-talkies and coffee machines to telephones and furniture), keep notes of when and how everything gets returned. Draft a memo combining all these notes and send it to the Producer, Production Manager, Production Accountant, and to yourself. Also note last

218

working dates for all the office staff, and the status of issues that could not be completed by the end of your last workday. This memo will be a wonderful reference after your departure.

4. List Items For Sale

Note everything that production bought and each item's original purchase price. Other production companies just starting up will buy pretty much everything from folding tables to office supplies. Approve and price the sale list with the Production Manager, then contact other Production Coordinators to peddle your goods.

5. Wardrobe Department and Set Department Sales

Unless the production is a television series that must store its wardrobe, sets, and props for future episodes, the Wardrobe and Set Dressing Departments will hold a sale of their goods, too. Find out when the sales are planned and coordinate the office sale simultaneously. This will help attendance.

6. Crew Gifts Delivered and Distributed

Whether they are hats, bags, sweatshirts, pins, watches or bathmats with the show title on them, make sure the crew gifts are delivered in time. Keep in touch with the supplier. The Producer may want them handed out on the last day of principal photography or at the wrap party.

MAKE LABELS FOR DISTRIBUTION

Handing out crew gifts sounds easy until you see the mountainous heap of crew gifts left on the office floor from the courier. If you have 200 sweat shirts to hand out, some will go to the set crew, some to the post–production crew, some to cast that wrapped weeks ago, and some to executives in another country. It is very easy to give too many gifts to one person, and run out before you have finished. If the gift is free, many crew members will ask you for an extra one or two for their families and friends. Just like scripts, label each gift before distribution. You have a list of who is entitled to a crew gift. On file folder labels, write one crew name per label (include size, if applicable). Then preorganize the labels in groupings of: (1) those to be couriered out of country; (2) those to be delivered around town; (3) those to be distributed on set; and (4) those who are coming into the office to pick them up.

When the stacks of crew gifts arrive, slap a label on each one. Done. If not, have several spare gifts on hand, because those 200 identical sweatshirts after distribution on set are just that: identical. Some will get lost. Some people will take two.

MAKE BOXES FOR DISTRIBUTION

Though the crew gifts are labeled, they still may be a large bundle to handle. Decorate old photocopier paper boxes with wrapping paper and put the crew gifts into the boxes in roughly alphabetical order (i.e., clump all the A's together in any order). Then label the boxes with the appropriate letters. Now you can hand out the gifts, or let the crew pick them up on their own.

WHEN CREW GIFTS ARE A SURPRISE

It is next to impossible to keep a surprise from an entire crew. If you want to try, use a code word with the supplier on the telephone to inform him/her that you cannot talk presently because someone else is in the room. On arrival, whisk the crew gifts into a predesignated solitary room (with a lock) to store, label, and box them in private. You can also encourage a red herring rumor to steer the crew offtrack in guessing what the gifts might be.

WHEN HANDING OUT FREE GIFTS ON THE LAST DAY OF SHOOTING

Check with the Producer if the daily crew and daily cast on the last day should receive a crew gift. Know the company's position before being put on the spot when someone asks.

WHEN "CREW GIFTS" ARE PURCHASED BY THE CREW

Purchased crew gifts are not really "gifts" at all, but "gift" is the only term that covers such a wide range of items. Review the choices and prices with the Production Manager, and decide on an item or two. Make and distribute a flyer to the crew presenting all the information necessary, including a picture or drawing if you can. Get payment in advance, or ask Accounting if paycheck deductions can be effected. Keep a separate file to track the orders and money. Because of the number of people involved and the sporadic way the money will filter in, this job will become very time-consuming. Be prepared.

7. *Crew Photograph*

A crew photo may be taken on the last day, or during the shoot and copied for distribution on the last day. Distribute these the way you do crew gifts (with labels).

8. *Get Final Invoices*

Now that you are emptying the office, telephone your suppliers to ask for final invoices immediately, especially suppliers to the wrap party. Have them fax the invoices so that payment can be effected while you are still in the office to make sure it happens.

9. *Close Accounts*

Check with the Production Manager which accounts are to be closed (from the office cleaners to the water delivery). Fax letters to those suppliers confirming that the account has been closed because production is completed. Copy these letters to Accounting and file them in the wrap file. The courier account should remain active for use during Post–Production. Send the remaining blank waybills to Accounting and/or to the Post–Production Supervisor.

10. *Be Careful Ordering Office Supplies In Wrap*

Double–check the crew requests for office supplies as you get close to wrap. You will be ordering many storage boxes, but should not be ordering staplers and rulers. Ensure that production does not furnish crew home offices.

11. *Box Up Files for Head Office*

The filing cabinet is currently filled with reams of paperwork. As you box up the files for storage at head office, make a point of looking through each file one by one. Pull out any duplicate or extraneous material. You may find that up to one third of the paper in the filing cabinet is expendable. Label each file box clearly with the title, your title, and the date. Include a disk of all your computer files that relate to the project (identifying the software you used on the label). Finally, find out the name of the person to receive these files at head office. Have the Office P.A. personally deliver the file boxes to that person. These files are important. They tell head office everything that happened on the production.

12. Forward Telephone To Head Office

When arranging for the telephone disconnection, forward the telephone number to the head office number. This helps people trying to find the company in a month or two.

13. When You Do Not Have To Empty the Office To Bare Walls

If the office is a permanent production office, or if another production company is moving in when you are done, you may not have to empty the office down to the bare walls. You are lucky. With the Production Manager, decide what part of the office can be emptied or simplified, then do a scaled-down version of wrap.

14. Take Your Kit Home

At the end of your last day, take home your kit. The longer you are on production the more you will have brought in during the past weeks or months, so make sure the Office P.A. is still around to give you a hand.

15. Hand In Your Keys

Very last, hand in your office keys to the Production Manager, or whomever is left in the office.

B. THE WRAP PARTY AND INTERACTIVE BUDGET FORM

Though the wrap party is not the very last thing you do in wrap, it does signify the end of production; therefore, here it is addressed last.

THE UNEDITED INVITATION LIST

Start with all the lists (crew, cast, credit, and contact lists) to create a mega, first draft invitation list to the wrap party. Include absolutely everyone you can think of so that you do not forget a soul. This list will be enormous.

SEE POTENTIAL PARTY VENUES

In conjunction with creating the invitation list, research places to hold the party. Visit these venues. Just like hotel rooms, there is nothing like seeing the place in person to make discussing the party location easier.

FIRST DISCUSSIONS WITH THE P.M.

Review the first draft invitation list with the Production Manager and narrow it down to reality. Decide if spouses and guests are invited. Decide on a day of the week, and discuss possible venues. Get an idea of the money you are allowed to spend.

WRAP PARTY BUDGET

It is your turn to generate a budget and track the costs. Make the wrap party come in on budget, but with flare. Use the following interactive checklist to prepare the wrap party budget.

WRAP PARTY CHECKLIST and BUDGET

Date of party:

INVITATIONS

You can create invitations on the photocopier, or convince the Art Department to design invitations for professional printing. Decide if you will fax, mail, or deliver invitations. Invitations that people have to surrender at the door (for door prizes) are great both to ensure that people bring them, and to cut down on gate–crashers.

	Description/Notes	Price
Number invited		
Invitation costs		
Mailing costs		

PARTY ROOM

Make sure the room is big enough for the crowd. Note down the features of the room, like a fireplace or billiard tables. These features may help sway you on choice of venue. Rental is usually free if a bar is supplied with the room. Know when you have to vacate at the end of the evening. Estimate the costs involved of supplying washroom supplies and/or a cleaning service. Find out if you or the venue will supply security.

	Description/Notes	Price
Room rental		
Capacity		
Special features		
Closing time		
Security		
Washroom supplies		
Cleanup		

DECOR OF ROOM

Is the lighting appropriate for the party? You may want to arrange lights from your equipment supplier or buy miniature Christmas lights to create a mood. Decide how many tables and chairs you will need and price their rental. Table cloths and ashtrays are often supplied by the caterer if you ask for them. Some decoration ideas to spark your imagination are helium balloons strung onto film cores, film cans as ashtrays, and, of course, flowers. Budget some money to hire a Production Assistant or two to help you with the setup and to do the cleanup. You will be busy enough hosting the party to have any time to "work" the party as well. Hire Assistants who have not worked on the show until now so that they will not be tempted to drink and socialize with the cast and crew.

	Description/Notes	Price
Lights rental		
Tables/Chairs		
Linen/Ashtrays		
Balloons/Helium		
Flowers		

CATERING

Decide what food you want to serve. Will you have a serve-yourself buffet of pizza or oysters shucked by catering staff? Order food for 60 percent of the attendees, as people do not eat as much as they drink at parties. For dessert, a cake with the film title in icing looks wonderful. To ensure that people will actually eat the cake rather than just admire it all evening, arrange for the Producer (or someone) to cut the cake, then arrange for other people to physically hand the slices out. The caterer can supply napkins, plates, and cutlery for this purpose. Will you use paper plates or the real thing? Confirm when the caterer needs access to the room for setup, and when they will return to clean up.

	Description/Notes	Price
Food/buffet type		
Specialty food		
Catering staff		
Cake		
Napkins (type)		
Plates (type)		
Cutlery (type)		
Setup/Cleanup		

BAR

Are you arranging for your own bar or will you use the room's bar? If you choose the room's bar, discuss the prices and deposit. Buy wine by the bottle instead of by the glass if you can. Decide how many bartenders you will need. Who is getting the ice and ice containers? If you choose a full bar (beer, wine, and liquor), who is getting the mixers? The caterer can supply you with more napkins and glasses if you ask. Know who is in charge of setting up and cleaning up the bar.

	Description/Notes	Price
Bartenders		
Deposit required		
Beer		
Wine		
Liquor		
Mixers & others		
Ice & containers		
Glasses (type)		
Napkins & access.		
Setup/cleanup		

LICENSE

If you arrange for your own bar, you need a "no sale" liquor license. You cannot charge money for the drinks. Contact your local licensing office for the procedure and fee.

	Description/Notes	Price
Liquor license		

NOTIFICATIONS

To have a large party, you should also notify the police, the fire department, health department, and buildings & inspections department. You may need these letters to complete your liquor license application. They do not cost anything and you can fax or deliver them. You are showing these departments that you know how to run a safe party and when you are going to do it. Include in each letter when, where, how many guests, describe security, mention that you will be serving food, and explain that the party is an end-of-production party.

	Description/Notes	Price
Police		
Fire Department		
Health Department		
Build'g/Inspect'n		

MUSIC

Will you have a band or a disk jockey? If a band, confirm that they are providing their own lights and equipment. Ask if they can supply recorded music in between sets. Be clear when the music is to start and to end. Discuss with the band or disk jockey how they may feel about a possible extension to the end of the evening if the party is going well. Ask when they need access to the room for setup and cleanup.

	Description/Notes	Price
Band		
D.J.		
Setup needed		
When cleanup		

OTHER ENTERTAINMENT

Other entertainment could be door prizes, or access to a skating rink, the showing of an outtake reel, or whatever your imagination can dream up. If you choose an outtake reel, give the editors enough time to complete one. When you rent the equipment to show it, hire enough technicians to take care of the setup, testing, and cleanup of the equipment.

	Description/Notes	Price
Entertainment type		
Outtake reel avail		
Video equipment		
Setup/cleanup		

TOTAL

Approve the party choices and prices with the Production Manger. Total the budget and copy it for the P.M., the Production Accountant, and yourself. You have to monitor and keep to these costs.

GRAND TOTAL PARTY COSTS:

HOST THE PARTY

Now that the party is budgeted, arranged, and happening, you step into the shoes of host. Be available so that your "party" Production Assistants can find you if they need you. Socialize and welcome everyone. But above all else, have a great time! This is your party too! You deserve it.

After the wrap party night, you return to the office to complete wrapping the office. The hours slow down again and you adjust to the pace of wrap. Around the office you hear people rave about how wonderful a party it was. Smile. They have you to thank for it.

CLOSING NOTES

Congratulations! You have just coordinated a film production!

If you feel like you have just dealt with absolutely everyone and everything during the course of making the film, you are right. You have. Coordinating can be a stressful experience. When the stress gets to you, remember this: it is only a movie. Take a deep breath and try to relax. You do not have to be an expert. You have the ability and you are prepared. You can carry on.

Take the time to meet the crew. Go to set when you can and keep in touch with the film. Production coordinating is more than shuffling paperwork. It is one critical part of the magical wheel of making a film come to life. Learn everything you can. Ask questions.

Use this book to create your own style of organization. The job is now yours. Through production coordinating, you embark on a very exciting filmmaking adventure. It's an adventure that you can do more than survive. Make the most of it. "Now" will never happen again. So, enjoy every minute from prep all the way to post.

```
Production Company Ltd.                              Parent Company Ltd.
Production Company address                          Parent Company Address
Production Company phone and fax              Parent Company phone and fax

Co-Production Company Ltd.                          Funding Company Ltd.
Co-Production Company address                      Funding Company Address
Co-Production Company phone and fax          Funding Company phone and fax
```

CREW LIST

GREEN REVISED   3 Dec 2001

```
executive producer          NAME                        office phone #
                            c/o Company name

executive in charge         NAME                        office phone #
of production               c/o Company name

supervising producer        NAME                        office phone #
                            c/o Company name

associate producer          NAME                        office phone #
                            c/o Company name

producer                    NAME                          home phone #
                            home address

line producer               NAME                          home phone #
                            home address


director                    NAME                          home phone #
                            home address
                            Agent: Agency & address      agency phone #
                            Agent's name                   agency fax #

writer                      NAME                          home phone #
                            home address
                            Agent: Agency & address      agency phone #
                            Agent's name                   agency fax #
```

Continuing with home addresses and phone numbers, pager numbers and fax numbers:

PRODUCTION OFFICE
production manager
assistant production manager
production coordinator
production secretary
office P.A.
assistant to producer
tutor

ACCOUNTING DEPARTMENT
production accountant
assistant accountant

CASTING DEPARTMENT
casting director (leads)
casting director (on location)
extras casting

PUBLICITY
publicist
stills photographer

PRODUCTION - ON SET
1st assistant director
2nd assistant director
2nd 2nd assistant director
3rd assistant director
set production assistant
continuity supervisor

LOCATION DEPARTMENT
location manager
assistant location manager
location assistant

ART DEPARTMENT
production designer
art director
1st assistant art director
2nd assistant art director
computer graphics
draftsman
storyboard artist

SETS DEPARTMENT
set decorator
lead set dresser
set dresser
on-set set dresser

PROPS DEPARTMENT
property master
lead props
props buyer

VISUAL EFFECTS
effects supervisor
computer animation
special effects
prosthetics

WARDROBE DEPARTMENT
costume designer
assistant costume designer
wardrobe mistress
assistant wardrobe mistress
seamstress

HAIR/MAKEUP DEPARTMENT
hair designer
makeup artist

CAMERA DEPARTMENT
director of photography
camera operator
1st assistant camera
2nd assistant camera
camera department trainee

SOUND DEPARTMENT
sound recordist
boom operator

ELECTRICAL DEPARTMENT
gaffer
best boy
electric
generator operator

GRIP DEPARTMENT
key grip
dolly grip
grip

STUNTS DEPARTMENT
stunt coordinator

TRANSPORTATION DEPARTMENT
transport coordinator
picture vehicle coordinator
transport captain
head driver
driver

CATERING/CRAFT SERVICE
caterer
craft service

CONSTRUCTION DEPARTMENT
construction manager
head carpenter
carpenter
scenic painter
construction labour

POST-PRODUCTION
post production supervisor
music composer
picture editor
assistant editor
sound effects editor
dialogue editor

231

(On Letterhead)

"Script Revision Nightmare"

<u>CAST LIST</u>

BLUE REVISED - 2 Dec 2001

1. Coordinator   ACTOR'S NAME   Talent Agency
                                   Home address   (Agent's Name)
                                   Home phone   Agency address
                                                                 Agency phone
                                                                  Agency fax

2. Compy's Voice   STAR'S NAME   Talent Agency/Manager
                                   c/o Hotel   (Agent/Manager Name)
                                   Hotel address   Agency address
                                   Hotel phone   Agency phone
                                                                 Agency fax

3. Friend   ACTOR'S NAME   Talent Agency
                                   Home address   (Agent's Name)
                                   Home phone   Agency address
                                                                 Agency phone
                                                                  Agency fax

4. Little Boy   ACTOR'S NAME   Talent Agency
                                   Home address   (Agent's Name)
                                   Home phone   Agency address
                                   (Parent's names)   Agency phone
                                                                  Agency fax

<u>STUNTS</u> - Stunt Agency, address, phone & fax

51. Stunt Coordinator   STUNT PERFORMER NAME   Home phone
                                         Home address

<u>STAND-INS</u>

Female Stand-in   STAND-IN'S NAME   Home phone
                                      Home address

Male Stand-in   STAND-IN'S NAME   Home phone
                                      Home address

N.B. Character numbers match A.D. character number assignments (i.e., on all schedules and call sheets).

"Script Revision Nightmare"

Contact List

PINK REVISED   4 December 2001

Air Conditioning   Company Name   Telephone #
                          Address   Fax #
                          Contact Person

Apartment Rental   Company Name   Telephone #
                          Address   Fax #
                          Contact Person

Batteries   Company Name   Telephone #
                          Address   Fax #
                          Contact Person
                          Account #

Continuing with this format, list suppliers, contact names, and
account numbers for the following subjects:

Casting Facility

Cel Phones

Cleaners

Coffee Machine/Supplies

Computer Rental

Conference Operator

Courier (in town)

Courier (international)

Customs Broker

Doctor

Disposal & Containers

Drafting Equipment

Electrian

Equipment (camera/grip/elec.)

Equipment (scaffolding)

Expendables (gels, etc.)

Film Stock	Script Research Company
Florist	Security
Funding Agencies	Stock Footage
Furniture Rental	Studio
Guarantor Company	Tables & Chairs Rental
Hotel	Taxi
Immigration	Telephone Rental
Limousine	Telephone: Long Distance
Location Supplies	Towel Service
Music Rights Clearances	Travel Agent
Moving & Storage Company	Tutors
Nurses	Unions & Guilds
Office Rental	Vehicle Rental
Office Supplies	Vehicles: Honeywagons
Pagers	Vehicles: Winnies
Payroll Service	Vehicles: Winnie pump-out
Photocopier & Fax Machine	Vehicles: Road/Traffic Info
Photofinishing	Vehicles: Tow Truck/Repairs
Plumber	Video Rental
Post: Laboratory	Video Stock
Post: Editing Facility	Walkie-Talkies
Post: Sound Editing Facility	Wardrobe Supplier/Builder
Post: Video Transfers	Washer/Dryer
Printing Company	Water Machine
Product Placement	Weather Information
Recycling	
Safety Supplies	

LETTER OF AGREEMENT

between:

PRODUCTION COMPANY LTD.   AND   CATERING COMPANY LTD.
Production Company Address   Catering Company Address
Production Company Telephone   Catering Company Telephone
Production Company Fax   Catering Company Fax

Date

This is to confirm that Catering Company Ltd. ("The Caterer") agrees to cater "Script Revision Nightmare" Television Movie for Production Company Ltd. ("The Production") for the period: Start Date - End Date .

The Caterer agrees to provide meals for cast and crew for   Price   plus tax per person and substantials for   Price   plus tax per person.

In addition, The Caterer will provide their own vehicle.

The Production agrees to supply tables and chairs and all beverages.

The Production agrees to provide The Caterer with a deposit of Amount.

With regard to changes in location, meal time and number of meals to be served, The Production agrees to give The Caterer best effort for twenty four (24) hours notice.

Invoices to be submitted weekly.

Signed and agreed,

_____   _____
Production Manager   Name:
on behalf of   on behalf of
PRODUCTION COMPANY LTD.   CATERING COMPANY LTD.

_____   _____
Date   Date

<u>"Script Revision Nightmare"</u>

Version #1 Credits - 4th Draft

December 15, 2001

OPENING CREDITS

<u>CARD #</u>

1	Script Revision Nightmare
2	Actor
3	Actor
4	Actor
5	Actor
6	and Actor Name as Character Name
7	Written by
8	Directed by

<u>"Script Revision Nightmare"</u>   Credits Ver.1 -2

Version #1 Credits - 4th Draft

END CREDITS (CRAWL)

Executive Producer

Producer

Co-Producer

Director Of Photography

Production Designer

Costume Designer

Editor

Music

Featuring
(in alphabetical order)

Actor Name   as   Character Name
Actor Name   as   Character Name
Actor Name   as   Character Name
Actor Name   as   Character Name

With special thanks to
(List a few special names)

Associate Producer

Associate Director

Production Manager
First Assistant Director
Casting Director
Legal Advisor
Executive in Charge of Production

Production Coordinator
Assistant Coordinator
Production Accountant
Assistant Accountant

Production Secretary
Office P.A.
Assistant to the Producer

Unit Manager
Location Manager

Second Assistant Director
Second Second Assistant Director
Third Assistant Director
Continuity Supervisor

Camera Operator
Focus Puller
2nd Assistant Camera
Trainee

Gaffer
Best Boy
Electric
Generator Operator
Key Grip
Best Boy Grip
Grip
Sound Recordist
Boom Operator

Art Director
Set Decorator
Assistant Art Director
Trainee
Model Builder
Lead Set Dresser
Set Dressers
Property Manager
Props Assistant
Props Buyer

Construction Manager
Head Carpenter
Carpenters
Scenic Artist
Painters
Construction Labor

Assistant Wardrobe Designer
Wardrobe Mistress
Assistant Wardrobe
Seamstress
Hair Designer
Key Makeup Artist

Special Effects
Stunts
Location Casting
Extras Coordinator

Transportation Coordinator
Driver Captain
Drivers
Boat/Vehicle Wrangler

Post Production Supervisor
Second Editor
Assistant Editor
Negative Cutting
Color Timing
Laboratory

Sound Supervisor
Sound Effects Designer
Dialogue Editor
Sound Mixer
Sound Mix Facility

Music Director
Music Engineer
Soloist
Additional Vocals

Location Catering
Craft Service Company
Nurse
Unit Publicity
Stills Photographer
Titles Design

Filmed on (film stock)

The producers gratefully acknowledge
the support and assistance of

Produced by (Co-Production Companies)

A (list countries) Co-Production

Produced with the participation of

Produced in association with

Developed with the assistance of

(Legal disclaimer, ie:
This film is based on true events, however, some of the names in this
film were changed and some events fictionalized for dramatic purposes.
This motion picture is protected under the laws of the United States,
Canada and other countries, and its unauthorised duplication,
distribution or exhibition may result in civil liability or criminal
prosecution.)

© (year, in Roman numerals) Production Company Ltd.

(Union and Guild logos)

(Co-Production Companies logos)

<u>"SCRIPT REVISION NIGHTMARE"</u>

Version #2 Credits

EPISODE #2 - "Oh no! Not Again!"

<u>Opening Credits</u>

<u>FONT STYLE</u>: VENETIAN 521 GOUDY EXTRA BOLD

Final Draft - 20 Dec 2001

<u>Card #</u>

1   Script Revision Nightmare

2   starring
Lead Actor

3   Lead Actor

4   and Lead Actor as Character Name

5   series created by

6   based on characters by
developed for television by

7   supervising producer

8   producer

<u>Shown over the first frames of Act One</u>:

9   Oh No! Not Again!

10   written by

11   directed by

"SCRIPT REVISION NIGHTMARE"   Credits Ver.2 - 2

Version #2 Credits

EPISODE #2 - "Oh no! Not Again!"

Tail Credits

Final Draft

Card #

1   executive producer

2   executive in charge of production

3   guest starring
        Star Name   as   Character Name
                    and featuring
        Actor Name   as   Character Name

4   director of photography
                   production designer

5   editor
                         music
                       theme by
                     performed by

6   casting director
                   wardrobe designer

7   production manager
            assistant production manager
               first assistant director
              second assistant director
               third assistant director
                continuity supervisor

8   art director
            1st assistant art director
            1st assistant art director
               art department trainee
                   set decorator
                   lead set dresser
                   lead set dresser
                     set dresser

9   special effects design
                     props master
                     props builder
                    props assistant
              art department coordinator

10
camera operator
1st camera assistant
2nd camera assistant
camera department trainee
sound mixer
boom operator

11
assistant wardrobe designer
wardrobe mistress
makeup artist
hair designer

12
key grip
dolly grip
gaffer
best boy
construction manager
head carpenter
scenic painter

13
production coordinator
production accountant
business affairs
production secretary
production assistant
craft service
catering

14
post-production supervisor
post-production coordinator
post-production assistant
sound editors
1st assistant editor
foley artist
sound assistant

15
rerecording
laboratory
rerecording studio
post-production facilities
on line editor
colorist
sound editing facility

16
© (Year) Production Company Ltd.
(Disclaimer) (Piracy Clause)
(Union and Guild logos)

17
Produced with the participation of

18
produced by
in association with

19
Co-Production Company logos

Production Company Ltd.
Production Company Address
Production Company Phone
Production Company Fax

Purchase Order No. ___001___

To: **SUPPLIER COMPANY** **SUPPLIER ADDRESS** **SUPPLIER PHONE** **SUPPLIER FAX**	Ship to: **STUDIO** **STUDIO ADDRESS** **CONTACT PERSON**
Contact Name: **PERSON NAME**	Delivery Date: **7 DEC 2001**
Ordered by: **DEBORAH**	Tax #: **ATTACHED EXEMPTION FORM**
Date ordered: **5 DEC 2001**	Terms: **INVOICE**

Qty	Description	Unit	Total
5	**REALLY NECESSARY ITEMS (RENTAL)**	7.50/DAY	225.00
	2 WEEK RENTAL (3-DAY WEEK)		
	DELIVERY TO STUDIO		N/C
	PICK UP FROM _OFFICE_ ON 21 DEC 2001		N/C
	RE: LOCATION DEPARTMENT		
Approval: *WJP*			**225.00**

Copy - Supplier   Copy - Production Company   Copy - Accounting

		Sc.#	1	14		26	11	6	
		Day/Night	N	D		D	D	D	
		Int/Ext	Int	Int		Int	Ext	Ext	
		Day #	1	2		3	2	3	
		Pages	1 1/8	1 4/8		1/8	2/8	2/8	
Title: Script N'mare Director: Jane Doe Producer: John Smith A.D.: John Doe Script date: Pink			OFFICE	OFFICE	Day 1 - End - 2 5/8 pages	KITCHEN	DRIVEWAY	TERRY'S HOUSE	Day 2 - End - 4/8 pages
Character	Artist	No.							
Terry		1	1	1		1	1	1	
Compy V/O		2	2-vo	2-vo					
Friend #1		3				3			
Friend #2		4							
Roommate		5				5			
Thug		6					6		
Mother		7				7-vo			
Father		8							
		9							
		10							
		11							
		12							
Spot (dog)		13					13		
		14							
Extras		X					X	X	
			Compy introduces self with flare	A truce is called - Terry hopes		Cooking experiments/Mom calls	Make friends with thug... not dog	All's quiet coming home	

BREAKDOWN SHEET #	SCRIPT BREAKDOWN SHEET	SCENE #
28	FILM TITLE: **SCRIPT REVISION NIGHTMARE**	23

INT / EXT	SET **COORDINATOR'S KITCHEN**	DAY / NIGHT N-4	PAGES 2 3/8

DESCRIPTION **COORD. DESPERATELY TRIES TO MAKE DINNER**	LOCATION	STUDIO **STUDIO 1**

CAST	EXTRAS	STUNTS
1. COORDINATOR	STAND-IN FOR COORD.	51. STUNT-COORDINATOR COORD. SLIPS ON BANANA PEEL CRASH PAD

PROPS	WARDROBE	VEHICLES
LOTS OF COOKING POTS,	DOUBLES FOR STUNT,	
BLACKENED FOOD,	NEVER-USED APRON,	
NON-SLIP BANANA PEEL,	NEVER-USED OVEN MITTS	
SMOKE IN OVEN,		

PROPS (continued):

BRIEFCASE,

COMPUTER IN BAG,

PENS & PENCILS (TO FALL OUT OF BRIEFCASE),

PHOTO OF JAMES

NOTES

ANIMALS: BIRD AT WINDOW WATCHES THE MESS, WRANGLER

ELECTRICS: DAY FOR NIGHT

NOTE TO ALL: SMOKE IN OVEN

MAKEUP: COORDINATOR LOOKS VERY, VERY TIRED

"SCRIPT REVISION NIGHTMARE"   CALL SHEET   Day: 11
Production Company Inc.   Date: MONDAY 29 OCTOBER 2001
Office #: 555-1212
                                     BREAKFAST READY: 0630
Producer/Director: (Name)   LEAVE FOR SET: 0730
Production Manager: (Name)
Assistant Director: (Name)   On Location: 0800
                                      Shooting Call: 0915
LOCATION: MAPS HANDED OUT AT BREAKY   Lunch: 1300

WEATHER: Cloudy, windy, light rain, hi:14, lo:6, POP:70%   SUNRISE/SET: 0749-1816

POLICE: (Telephone #)   AMBULANCE: (Telephone #)   FIRE: (Telepone #)

SC#	SET	D/N	CAST	PGS	SYNOPSIS
***	*MORE "DRIVING & PROCESS" BLOCK SHOOTING THE FOLLOWING "TERRY CAR" SCENES*				***
8pt	INT TERRY'S CAR	Day	1.3.	6/8	Next day, same route
9pt	INT TERRY'S CAR	Day	1.3.	1 0/8	Friend has to give advice on sleep
10pt	INT TERRY'S CAR	Ev'g	1.3.	1 0/8	Magic hour: Arriving at work
15pt	INT FRIEND'S CAR	Night	3.	1/8	Friend looks for Terry
Reduced unit...					
26	INT FRIEND'S CAR	D4N	1.	---	Isn't that the same street sign?
Target of opportunity...					
1	INT TERRY'S CAR	Morng	1.3.	2/8	Gosh, ya gotta love these hours
2	INT TERRY'S CAR	Ev'g	1.	1/8	Home so soon?

☹ ☹ ☹ C L O C K S   G O   B A C K   O N E   H O U R   T O N I G H T ☹ ☹ ☹

CHARACTER	ARTIST		LV.COTT	H/M/W	SET
1. TERRY	(Name)		0730	0800	0900
3. FRIEND #1	(Name)		0730	0800	0900

SET REQUIREMENTS

VEHICLES   -Terry's car on tow rig for block shooting, then home for processing
                -Friend's car on set for "Flashlight scene"
                -Friend's car on standby for reduced unit
LIGHTING/GRIP 9:   Glare of sun passes
               10:   Door opens to beam of diffuse light, Car moves into sun
ART DEPT   8-10: Terry's littered car dressing
               8:    Bug splat on windshield
               9:    Friend's candies
               26:   Street sign: "The Middle of Nowhere"
MAKEUP/HAIR   15:   Terry looks haggard
WARDROBE   8:   Terry's gym clothes, Terry's watch
               9:    Terry's watch
               15:   Terry's gym shoe (left)
NOTES   26:   Dry ice

TUESDAY ADVANCE SCHEDULE   Cloudy windy cool hi:10 lo:2 POP:60%(0650-1714)

4	EXT TERRY HOUSE	Morng	---	1/8	Establishing shot
23	INT LIVING ROOM	Morng	1.	4/8	Trying to identify her own home
25	INT LIVING ROOM	Morng	1.	2/8	Terry passes out on the couch
24	INT KITCHEN	Morng	1.	3/8	Trying to identity the coffee pot
28	INT LIVING ROOM	Night	1.	2/8	Slept through the whole day?!?

Call sheet joke here...

```
"SCRIPT REVISION NIGHTMARE"    CALL SHEET    Day:  14
Film Company Inc.                            Date: WED., FEBRUARY 21, 2001
Address
Telephone                            CALL:  3:00am
Night Line Telephone          Gennie Op x2:  2:30am
                               Honeywagon:  2:30am
Exec. Producers     (Name)         MU/Hair:  3:00am
                    (Name)             Wdb:  2:30am
Producers           (Name)           Craft:  2:15am
                    (Name)     Substantials:  5:30am  No:85
Prdn. Manager       (Name)           Lunch:  9:00am  No:85  Box:300
Director            (Name)
                                   Sunrise:  7:08am
Episode #5 "I Live For Plaid"      Sunset:  5:56pm
                                   Weather:  sunny, windy, warmish
Set Cel: (Tel.#)                   POP 0%  Lo:-5  Hi:+5
Loc Cel: (Tel.#)    LOCATION: (SEE MAP)
                    1. Hockey Arena, (Address)
```

SC#	SET/DESCRIPTION	CAST	D/N	PGS	LOC
34-B	INT ICE SURFACE The dream-game	1,4,6,12,Black team x15, White team x12,Refs x3,Coach x1, Fans x298, Photographer x1	N10	3 4/8	1
34-F	INT STANDS Fans cheer them on	12,Fans x300	N10	1/8	1
34-A	INT BLACK BENCH But we're bad guys?	1,2(vo),4,6,Black team x15, Fans x300	N10	1 0/8	1
34-D	INT BLACK BENCH Somebody wake me?	1,2(vo),4,6,Black team x15, Fans x300	N10	3/8	1

```
* 2ND CAMERA DAY                              TOTAL: 5 0/8
```

CHARACTER	ARTIST	PU	H/M/W	SET	LOC
1 Terry	(Name)	3:15am	3:30am	4:00am	1
2 Compy V/O	(Name)	--	N/A	N/A	
4 Friend #2	(Name)	--	3:30am	4:00am	1
6 Thug	(Name)	--	3:30am	4:00am	1
12 Reporter	(Name)	--	3:00am	4:00am	1

```
PHOTO DOUBLES
```

		PU	H/M/W	SET	LOC
1A Terry Double		--	2:30am	3:00am	1
4A Friend Double		--	2:30am	3:00am	1
6A Thug Double		--	2:30am	3:00am	1

```
EXTRAS
```

	PU	H/M/W	SET	LOC
Cast of thousands! ... uh, hundreds! Fans x298	--		4:00am	1
Coach x1, Photographer x1	--		4:00am	1
Black team x15, White Team x12		2:30am	3:00am	1
Refs x3		3:00am	4:00am	1

```
1st AD:(Name/Phone)    2nd AD:(Name/Phone)    Transport:(Name/Phone)
```

DAILY CREW
2:30am - P.A. Daily x1, TAD Daily x1 to report to set.
3:00am - 2nd Camera x1, 2nd Focus Puller x1 to report to set.

TRANSPORTATION
2:30am - Honeywagon hot and cooking!
3:15am - Transport to pick up "Terry" at the hotel

ADVANCE SCHEDULE - DAY 15 - THURSDAY, FEBRUARY 22, 2001

30	INT ARENA STANDS	1,4	D9		4/8	1
45-A	INT STANDS	12,Fans x35	N11	1	0/8	1
45-C	INT STANDS	Fans x35	N11		1/8	1
45-B	INT WHITE BENCH	1,2(vo),4,7,Fans x35	N11		7/8	1
35	INT ARENA CORRIDOR	1,2(vo),7	N10		1/8	1

RUSHES OF DAY 13
4:30pm - at the Lab

Crew Rep: (Name)   Actor's Union: (Name/Phone)   Safety Rep: (Name)

Callsheet joke here...

Map to location (with closest hospital noted) here...

DEAL MEMORANDUM

BETWEEN: Prdn. Company: _____
            _____

AND: Company/Name: _____
            Address: _____
            _____

            Telephone: _____

            Co.Tax#/Soc.#: _____

****

CONCERNING THE FOLLOWING FILM PRODUCTION:

            _____

****

CATEGORY: _____

SHOOT DATES: _____

PAY RATE: PER DAY: _____

            OTHER: _____
                            _____

PAYABLE BY: INVOICE: _____   PAYROLL: _____

****

_____   _____
Company/Employee   on behalf of
                                    Production Company

_____   _____
Date   Date

ACCIDENT REPORT	
Date of Accident:	Time of Accident:
Date/Time Reported:	By Whom:
Description of Location:	
Injured Person (Full Name):	
Age:	Occupation:
Address:	Telephone:
Nature/Extent of Injuries:	
Attending Physician:	Address:
First Aid Rendered: Y / N	By Whom:
Hospital Name:	Conveyance (Name):
Witnesses Names/Addresses:	
Description of Incident:	
Reported by:	Signature:

Production Company Ltd.
TIME SHEET

Soc.#:_____

Name/Company:_____

Address:_____

Rate:_____ FOR WEEK ENDING:_____

Approvals:

Exec.Prd:_____ P.M.:_____

Dept.Head:_____ Acct.:_____

DAY	CALL	LUNCH		DINNER		WRAP	HRS	ST	1.5	2.0	2.5	3.0	MP	TA	HRS
SUN															
MON															
TUE															
WED															
THU															
FRI															
SAT															

TOTAL HOURS WORKED:

EQUIVALENT ST HOURS:

NOTES:

ITEM	ACCOUNT	AMOUNT
AMOUNT PAID:		

251

Production Company Ltd.
Production Company Address
Production Company Phone & Fax

CHECK REQUISITION

Date:_____ Required:_____ Amount/Currency:_____

PAYABLE TO: _____

                 _____

                 _____

                 _____

TELEPHONE: _____

CONTACT: _____

FOR: _____

                 _____

Mail Check:_____   Hold for P/U:_____   Give Check to:_____

APPROVALS:

Dept. Head:_____   P.M.:_____   Allocation:_____

Do not write below this line - for Accounting use only
****

Petty Cash Report

Name:_____ Film Title:_____

Dept.:_____ Date:_____

#	DATE	TO WHOM	PURPOSE	ACCT	NET AMT	TAX	TOTAL
1							
2							
3							
4							
5							
6							
7							
8							
9							
10							
11							
12							

APPROVALS		TOTALS:		
EX.P:	P.M.:	MINUS ADVANCE:		
DEPT:	ACCT:	BALANCE/DUE:		

DISTRIBUTION:					

Film Title: P.O. LOG   Page:

PO#	To Whom	For What	Ep#	Dept	Date	Amt

Film Title: COPIER PAPER COUNT   Page:

Date	white	pink	blue	green	yellw	gold	purpl	LEGAL	11x17	no-hole
Fri.										
Fri.										
Fri.										
Fri.										
Fri.										
Fri.										
Fri.										
Fri.										
Fri.										
Fri.										
Fri.										
Fri.										
Fri.										
Fri.										
Fri.										
Fri.										
Fri.										
Fri.										

Film Title: POLAROID FILM SIGN-OUT Page:

Date	Name	Department	Ep#	600 Taken	Spectra Taken

Film Title: WALKIE-TALKIE SIGN-OUT   Page:

Name/ Dept.	Walkie #	Serial #	Accessories	Date Taken	Date Return	Sign

BREAKDOWN SHEET #	**SCRIPT BREAKDOWN SHEET**	SCENE #
	FILM TITLE:	

INT / EXT	SET		DAY / NIGHT	PAGES

DESCRIPTION		LOCATION	STUDIO

CAST	EXTRAS	STUNTS

PROPS	WARDROBE	VEHICLES
	NOTES	

DAILY PRODUCTION REPORT - Prdn Company:　　　　　　　　DAY _____ of _____

Title: _____　　　　Date: _____
Producer/Director: _____　　　　Scheduled Dates: _____

Sets: _____
Locations: _____

Weather: _____

Crew Call- _____　Lunch- _____　Wrap - _____
#1 Shot AM _____　#1 Shot PM _____

	Scenes	Pages		Minutes		Setups
Scene #'s	Script -		Prev -		Prev -	
	Taken Prev-		Today -		Today -	
	Today -		Total -		Total -	
Wildtracks	To Date -		Avg -		Avg -	
	To be taken-					
	Avg/Day -		Script Running Time _____			

#	Cast	Character	SWF	Call	Set	Lunch out	Lunch in	Wrap	Sound Stock Usage
									of
									Avg Total Film Use/Day:

Position	Crew Name	Set	Wrap	Lunch out	Lunch in	Film Stock Usage	B/W	100ASA	400ASA
Director						Received Previous			
Prdn Mgr						Received Today			
Loc Mgr						Total Received			
1st AD						Used Previous			
2nd AD						Used Today			
Continuity						Total Used			
DOP						On Hand			
1st A.Cam.						NOTES:			
2nd A.Cam.									
Gaffer									
Electric									
Key Grip									
Grip									
Sound									
Boom Op									
Art Dir									
Set Dec									
Prop Master									
Wardrobe									
Wdb Asst									
Hair/MU									
Photographer									
PA's						1st AD:	PM:		

Production Company:

DAILY PRODUCTION REPORT

MAIN UNIT DAYS: _____ of _____
2ND UNIT DAYS: _____ of _____
TOTAL DAYS: [_____] of [_____]

Title: _____   Date: _____
Producer: _____   Director: _____
Start Date: _____   Finish Date: _____

Sets: _____
Locations: _____

Weather:

Crew Call- [_____]   Lunch- [_____]   Wrap - [_____]
#1 Shot AM   #1 Shot PM

Script Running Time [_____]

	Scenes	Pages		Minutes		Setups
Script -			Prev -		Prev -	
Taken Prev-			Today -		Today -	
Today -			Total -		Total -	
To Date -						
To be taken-			Avg -		Avg -	

Scene #'s

Wildtracks

FILM USE		Prev	Today	Total
100 ASA	Gross			
	Print			
	NG			
	Waste			
400 ASA	Gross			
	Print			
	NG			
	Waste			

FILM INVENTORY	Total Rec'd	Today	Total Used	On Hand
100 ASA				
400 ASA				
GRAND TOTAL				

#	Cast	Character	SWF	Call	Wrap	Lunch out	Lunch in

SOUND 1/4	Prev -
	Today -
	Total -

Cash Extras	Wdb-Set	Wrap	Amt

Qty	Act/Per/App	Type of Extra	H/M/W	Set	Wrap	Lunch out	Lunch in

TOTAL AMT CASH EXTRAS:

Asst Director:

Prdn Mgr:

Director		Title:		
1st AD		Day:	Date:	
2nd AD		Prdn Coord	Gun Wrangler	
3rd AD		Coord Asst	Animals	
Set PA		Office PA	Wrangler	
Continuity		Art Director	Nurse	
Craft Serv		1st Asst Art	Ambl. Attend	
DOP		2nd Asst Art	Security	
Cam.Op		Art Trainee	Policemen	
1st A.C.		Set Dec	ETF	
2nd A.C		Lead Sets	Vehicles (list):	
Cam.Trainee		Set Dresser		
Gaffer		On Set Dress		
Best Boy		FX Super		
Electric		FX Asst		
Gennie Op.		3D Artists		
Key Grip		2D Artists		
Best Boy Grip		Computer Artist		
Grip		Prosthetics		
Sound Mixer		SPFX		
Boom Op		SPFX Asst	Pic.Vehicles:	
Props Master		Stunt Coord		
Lead Props		Stills Photog.		
Props Buyer		Post Super.	Substantials at:	x
Cost. Design		Editor	Lunches at:	x
Ast Cost.Des.		Asst Editor	Dinners at	x
Wdb Asst		DAILIES:		
Seamstress				
Hair Design				
MU Artist				
Trans Coord				
Trans Captain				
Drivers				

NOTES:

Deborah Patz is president of Golden Arrow Productions. Golden Arrow provides producing, management and organizational services to the film industry. It also offers seminars and workshops. For rates and information, please contact Ms. Patz at:

GOLDEN ARROW PRODUCTIONS LTD.

3222 Sprucehill Avenue
Burlington, Ontario, Canada
L7N 2G5

tel: 905-632-6073
email: gould80@ibm.net

262

C O N S U L T I N G

S E R V I C E S

MICHAEL WIESE PRODUCTIONS can help you think bigger, create new programs, expand your markets, develop product lines, find co-production partners, locate distributors, design marketing plans, and develop your unique pathway to success.

We have provided our consulting services to clients large and small including: **National Geographic Television, The Smithsonian Institution, WNET, KCET, PBS Home Video, Hanna-Barbera, Mystic Fire Video, The Apollo Theater, The American Film Institute, Buckminster Fuller Institute, Republic Home Video, King World Television** and numerous independent producers. For more information, please call Ken Lee.

CALL TODAY
1-800-379-8808

263

THE FIRST BOOK TO DIRECTLY ADDRESS FILM AND TELEVISION DIRECTORS ABOUT WORKING WITH ACTORS.

DIRECTING ACTORS
CREATING MEMORABLE PERFORMANCES
FOR FILM & TELEVISION
by Judith Weston

Directing Actors is a method for establishing collaborative relationships with actors, getting the most out of rehearsals, recognizing and fixing poor performances, and developing your actors' creativity.

Ms. Weston discusses what constitutes a good performance, what actors want from a director, what directors do wrong, script analysis and preparation, how actors work, and the director/actor relationship.

This book, based on the author's twenty years of professional acting and eight years of teaching Acting for Directors, is the first book to directly address film and television directors about working with actors.

"After living on movie sets for over fifteen years, Judith's class opened a door for me to an aspect of that creative process about which I had never really been aware—acting."

Ron Judkins, Production Sound Mixer
Jurassic Park, Schindler's List

"Judy's class made me better able to judge actors' performances."

Arthur Coburn, Editor
The Mask, Dominick & Eugene, Beverly Hills Cop

$26.95, approx. 300 pages, 6 x 8 1/4
ISBN: 0-941188-24-8
Availabe June 1996

THE TRICKS OF NO-BUDGET FILMMAKING!

PERSISTENCE OF VISION
AN IMPRACTICAL GUIDE TO PRODUCING
A FEATURE FILM FOR
UNDER $30,000
by John Gaspard &
Dale Newton

NEW !!

PERSISTENCE OF VISION reveals the treacherous and often humorous process of creating ultra-low-budget feature films for $30,000 or less. It includes practical information on writing the script, budgeting, raising financing, casting, putting together a crew, and dealing with distributors.

This step-by-step book is an invaluable tool for all ultra-low-budget and novice filmmakers and includes interviews with ultra-low-budget filmmakers and a large Appendix of essential forms and contracts.

When it comes to producing successful films on a shoestring, authors John Gaspard and Dale Newton know of what they speak. Together they created "Resident Alien" and "Beyond Bob," two critically-acclaimed ultra-low-budget features using the tactics and strategies outlined in this book.

$26.95, 450 pages, 40 illustrations & photos
ISBN: 0-941188-23-x

YOU'LL LEARN HOW TO:

- WRITE FOR A TINY BUDGET
- CREATE UNIQUE CHARACTERS
- MAKE PRACTICAL BUSINESS DECISIONS
- FIND INVESTORS
- BREAKDOWN A SCRIPT
- CAST
- CREATE LOW-BUDGET SPECIAL EFFECTS
- GET YOUR FILM OUT INTO THE WORLD

TO ORDER CALL 1-800-379-8808

Read the Hottest Book in Hollywood!!!

THE WRITER'S JOURNEY
MYTHIC STRUCTURE FOR
STORYTELLERS &
SCREENWRITERS
by Christopher Vogler

Find out why this book has become an industry wide best-seller and is considered **"required reading"** by many of Hollywood's top studios! THE WRITER'S JOURNEY reveals how master storytellers from Hitchcock to Spielberg have used mythic structure to create powerful stories which tap into the mythological core which exists in us all.

Writer's will discover a set of useful myth-inspired storytelling paradigms (i.e. *The Hero's Journey*) and step-by-step guidelines for plotting and character development. Based on the work of **Joseph Campbell**, THE WRITER'S JOURNEY is a **must** for writers, producers, directors, film/video students, and Joseph Campbell devotees.

Vogler is a script consultant who has worked on scripts for "The Lion King," "Beauty and the Beast" and evaluated over 6000 others.

"This book should come with a warning: You're going to learn about more than just writing movies–you're going to learn about life! The Writer's Journey is the perfect manual for developing, pitching, and writing stories with universal human themes that will forever captivate a global audience. It's the secret weapon I hope every writer finds out about."

> *- Jeff Arch,*
> Screenwriter, *Sleepless in Seattle*

$22.95 paper, ISBN 0-941188-13-2, 200 pages, 6 x 8

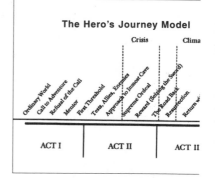

Another BEST-SELLER !
The most sought after book in Hollywood by top directors!!

FILM DIRECTING
SHOT BY SHOT
by Steven Katz

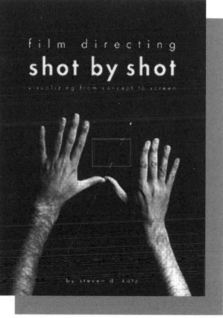

This best-seller is filled with
visual techniques for filmmakers and screenwriters to
expand their stylistic knowledge. With beautiful illustra-
tions and expertly written
directions, *Shot by Shot* has
been used as a reference tool
"on the set" by many of
Hollywood's directors.

Shot by Shot is a must for both
seasoned and novice filmmakers.
Includes **never before published** storyboards from Spielberg (*Empire of
the Sun*), Orson Welles (*Citizen Kane*), and Hitchcock (*The Birds*).

Katz is an award-winning filmmaker with over 20 years of experience in
the fields of writing, directing, and editing.

$24.95, ISBN 0-941188-10-8, 370 pages, 7 x 10, 750+ illus.

FILM DIRECTING: CINEMATIC MOTION
by Steven Katz

"...a valuable and relevant guide...(features) interesting interviews with film professionals."   *- 3D Artist*

This is a practical guide to common production problems encountered when staging and blocking film scenes. It includes discussions of scheduling, staging without dialogue, staging in confined spaces, actor and camera choreography in both large and small spaces, sequence shots, and much more. Interviews with well-known professionals–a cinematographer, a director, a production manager, a continuity person, and an actor–enhance this comprehensive study of stylistic approaches to camera space as they address the requirements of the production manager.

Katz is an award-winning filmmaker with over 20 years of experience in the fields of writing, directing, and editing.

$24.95, ISBN 0-941188-14-0, 200 pages, 7 x 10, illus.

PRODUCER TO PRODUCER
by Michael Wiese

"This book is like having a private consultation with Wiese. Invaluable information presented in a clear, concise manner."

Straight one-on-one talk from one of America's leading independent media producers. In 26 knockout chapters, you'll hear Wiese's latest thoughts on everything from program development, financing and production, to marketing, distribution and new media. Articles include: "Self-Distribution," "Infomercials: Where's the Info?," "Where Do You Get the Money?" and much more.

$24.95, ISBN 0-941188-15-9, 350 pages, 6 x 8 ¼

LATEST INDUSTRY INFORMATION--INSTANTANEOUSLY!!

FILM & VIDEO ON THE INTERNET

NEW !!

THE TOP 500 SITES
by Bert Deivert and
Dan Harries

Love film but over-whelmed by the Internet's maze of terrific (and not so terrific) information? Want to get to the good stuff fast and not spend needless hours searching for the treasures of film, video, and new media? Then this book is for you!

FILM & VIDEO ON THE INTERNET separates the wheat from the chaff by identifying and rating the top 500 film & video sites on the Internet.

This is an excellent book for film and videomakers, students, teachers and film buffs who are looking for the Internet's latest resources on film, video, and new media.

Each site is identified by name, its location on the Internet, category (such as "Directors" or "screenwriting"), a rating on its usefulness, and a brief review.

FILM & VIDEO ON THE INTERNET also includes helpful information about e-mail, newsgroups, the World Wide Web as well as a handy cross reference index for quick access.

$26.95, 400 pages, illustrations, 0-941188-54-x, *available April ' 96*

This FILM & VIDEO ON THE INTERNET diskette lets you point and click on your web browser so you can instantly go to the top 500 sites reviewed in this book.   You'll have a great database of resources available instantly. Only $29.

SAVE MONEY!! BOOK & DISKETTE BUNDLE: $49

TO ORDER CALL 1-800-379-8808

MAKE MONEY ON YOUR NEXT PRODUCTION!

FILM & VIDEO BUDGETS - 2ND EDITION
by Michael Wiese and Deke Simon

Now updated, revised and expanded, *Film & Video Budgets* includes detailed budget formats and sample budgets for many different kinds of productions –from film and tape documentaries to music videos, industrials and a $5 million feature–along with all the essential information that caused the first edition to sell over 30,000 copies.

Also includes such highly useful, new materials such as a comprehensive master list of line items which covers just about everything that could possibly be put into a production; and a new chapter on setting up a production company; a new chapter on pre-production, which includes such subjects as clip and music clearance, crew negotiations, and casting. Plus a killer appendix with money-saving ideas.

$26.95, ISBN 0-941188-22-1, 468 pages

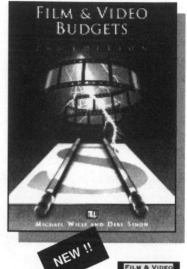

NEW !!

SAVE 12 %

FILM & VIDEO BUDGETS DISKETTE
for either the Mac or PC, uses Excel®, $29

SAVE MONEY! BOOK & DISKETTE BUNDLE: $49.
Save dozens of hours of inputting. All the budgets found in the book ready for you to customize for your own projects. An incredible value!

...rance		1	A...		9,...	3,...	
Overtime Allow		12	Days	1	300	3,600	37,
Second A.D.							
Prep/Travel		1.8	Weeks	1	2,406	4,331	
Shoot (incl. 6th day)		4	Weeks	1	2,406	9,624	
Prod. Fee		24	Days	1	119	2,856	
Severance		1	Allow	1	2,406	2,406	
Overtime		24	Days	1	201	4,812	
...-04 Production Coord							
Prep/T...		6	Weeks	1	1,200	7,200	
Shoot		...ks	1	1,200	4,800	
Wrap		...ks	1	1,200	2,400	1
Asst. Coord.							
Prep		6	Weeks	1	750	4,500	
Shoot		4	Weeks	1	750	3,000	
Wrap		1	Week	1	750	750	8,

OVER 40,000 SOLD PREVIOUS EDITION

ORDER FORM

To order these products please call 1-800-833-5738 or fax (818) 986-3408 or mail this order form to:

MICHAEL WIESE PRODUCTIONS
11288 Ventura Blvd., Suite 821
Studio City, CA 91604
1-818-379-8799

BOOKS:

_____
_____
_____
_____

Subtotal $ _____
Shipping $ _____
8.25% Sales Tax (Ca Only) $ _____

TOTAL ENCLOSED _____

Please make check or money order payable to
Michael Wiese Productions

(Check one) ____ Master Card ____ Visa ____ Amex

Company PO# _____

Credit Card Number _____
Expiration Date _____
Cardholder's Name _____
Cardholder's Signature _____

SHIP TO:

Name _____
Address _____
City _____ State _____ Zip _____
Country _____ Telephone _____
Ask about our free catalog

VISIT OUR HOME PAGE http://websites.earthlink.net/~mwp

Please allow 2–3 weeks for delivery.
All prices subject to change without notice.

CREDIT CARD ORDERS

CALL
1-800-833-5738

or FAX
818-986-3408

OR E-MAIL
mwpsales@earthlink.net

SHIPPING

UPS GROUND
One Book - $5.00
Two Books - $7.00
For each additional
book, add $2.00.

AIRBORNE EXPRESS
2nd Day Delivery
Add an additional
$11.00 per order.

OVERSEAS
Surface - $10.00 ea.
book
Airmail - $20.00 ea. book